GW00360929

A	Graye friers
B	St Pauls
C	Mary Magd
D	The Minster
E	St Margrets
F	St Michaells
G	The Castell
H	St Martins
K	St Laurence
L	St Peters arc
M	St Swithins
N	Black friers
O	Little Friers
P	Potter gat
Q	Ball gat
R	Clasket gat

Part of Lecester shire

THE BOOK OF LINCOLN

FRONT COVER: The Brayford Pool and Cathedral; a mid-Victorian view.

The Stonebow, Lincoln in 1836.

THE BOOK OF
LINCOLN

BY

IAN BECKWITH

BARRACUDA BOOKS LIMITED
BUCKINGHAM, ENGLAND
MCMXC

PUBLISHED BY BARRACUDA BOOKS LIMITED
BUCKINGHAM, ENGLAND

AND PRINTED BY
ALPHA PRINT (OXON) LIMITED
WITNEY, ENGLAND

BOUND BY
GREEN STREET BINDERY
OXFORD, ENGLAND

JACKETS PRINTED BY
CHENEY & SONS LIMITED
BANBURY, OXON

LITHOGRAPHY BY
SOUTH MIDLANDS LITHOPLATES LIMITED
LUTON, ENGLAND

TYPESET BY
KEYBOARD SERVICES
LUTON, ENGLAND

© Ian Beckwith 1990

All rights reserved. No part of this publication may be reproduced,
stored in a retrieval system, or transmitted, in any form or by any
means, electronic, mechanical, photocopying, recording or
otherwise, without the prior permission of Barracuda Books Limited.

Any copy of this book issued by the Publisher as clothbound or as a
paperback is sold subject to the condition that it shall not by way of
trade or otherwise, be lent, re-sold, hired out or otherwise circulated
without the Publisher's prior consent, in any form of binding or
cover other than that in which it is published, and without a similar
condition including this condition being imposed on a
subsequent purchaser.

ISBN 0 86023 441 X

Contents

Acknowledgements 8
Foreword by the Mayor of Lincoln 9
Introduction 11

Outpost of Empire 12
Free Under God 20
Power Politics 27
Monument of Love Divine 35
Greens and Scarlets 46
All God's Houses 59
The Moneymen 68
Pestilence, Famine and War 76
High Town, Low Town 83
Career of Prosperity 95
Wheels of Industry 107
Fit for Heroes 122

Select Bibliography 138
Index 139
Subscriptions 143

Acknowledgements

This book would not have been possible without the staff of Lincoln City Library, the Keeper of Art and his staff at the Usher Gallery, Lincoln, Chris Childs and the staff of the Sibthorpe Library, Bishop Grosseteste College, and the staff of the Bodleian Library, all of whom have dealt with my numerous requests with the utmost cheerfulness and courtesy. I am grateful to Christine Butler for drawing my attention to material in the Wass MSS in the library of Corpus Christi College, Oxford. My thanks also go to Ann Perfect for her help in tracking down the source of the photograph of the Roman army on the march and the Lincoln Mystery Play performance. The Mayor of Lincoln's Secretary, Julie Duxbury, has been most helpful in answering my queries and procuring photographs of the civic insignia and I am most grateful to the Right Worshipful the Mayor of Lincoln for writing the foreword. I am glad to be able to thank my friends Mary Phillips and Linda Tilbury for all their help. Most of all, to Ann-Marie who has been obliged to share the house and me with *The Book of Lincoln* for over a year, I owe a particular debt of thanks for her tolerance and support. Lastly, though it seems like an impertinence, this book is offered to the memory of a kindly friend, Sir Francis Hill, whose monumental history of Lincoln will be remembered wherever local historians gather. The shortcomings are, however, entirely mine.

Acknowledgements are made to the following for permission to reproduce material: the Dean and Chapter of Lincoln for *Magna Carta*; the Dean and Chapter of Hereford for the *Mappa Mundi*; the Bodleian Library for the *Gough Map*; the Imperial War Museum for the illustration of Tank No 1; the Usher Gallery for the reproduction of paintings by Joseph Baker, Peter De Wint, J.M.W. Turner, Frederick MacKenzie, John Ferneley, W.G. Herdman, George Pyne, Fred Lawson, and Nathan Drake; Gus da Cozar for the illustration of the final scene from Keith Ramsay's production of the Lincoln Cycle of Mystery Plays; the Public Record Office for the illustration of Aaron the Jew (E32/12, m.3d.) based on the picture in *Jewish Responses*, by Anthony Bayfield; the Crown copyright photograph of the earliest tank is reproduced by permission of the Trustees of the Imperial War Museum; the British Library for the Battle of Lincoln 1141, Arundel MS48, fo.168v, c1200; C.V. Middleton & Son for the photograph of the Mayor welcoming the Queen to Lincoln; Lincoln Civic Trust for the line drawings of The Chancery, no 18 Minster Yard, and the map of the Close and Town walls. All other illustrations are from the author's collection.

Foreword

by J.S. Robertson, Mayor of Lincoln 1989–90

Ever since arriving in the City of Lincoln forty years ago, I have been more than a little interested in the history of its buildings, its people, its origins and its way of life at the various stages of its existence and evolution. As the 783rd Mayor of Lincoln, I suppose I am now part of that history. My interest and curiosity has at times been fragmentary.

So it is with a sense of anticipation that I welcome an addition to the other accounts about Lincoln's history. A fresh account from another historian is always useful in understanding the heritage that rightly belongs to the present day inhabitants of such a city as Lincoln, with its long traditions of being an important settlement through the ages.

I commend Ian Beckwith's valuable contribution to understanding what has gone before in the making of the thriving, beautiful and historic City of Lincoln that I live in today.

J. S. Robertson

To write the story of a town
So ancient, and of such renown
As Lincoln, on her sovereign hill,
Would many bulky volumes fill.
Henry Winn of Fulletby

ABOVE: Lincoln as Daniel Defoe saw it. BELOW: In the early nineteenth century Lincoln still had a rural aspect.

Introduction

The intention of this book is to provide a summary of the history of Lincoln for the general reader in an easily accessible single volume. It is many years since such a book was published and an enormous amount of research, especially on the archaeology of the City, has added to and transformed our knowledge of Lincoln's past.

Two important caveats need to be made. Of necessity I have had to be selective and so it is easy to criticise *The Book of Lincoln* for its omissions. I am particularly aware of my brief treatment of twentieth century Lincoln. Secondly, I am deeply conscious of how much I have leaned upon other people's research work, most of all when it comes to the archaeology of the Roman, post-Roman and medieval city. I am extremely grateful therefore to the City of Lincoln Archaeological Unit, in particular to Mick Jones and John Wilford, for their patience and generosity, especially in freely allowing me to use illustrations from their publications, notably David Vale's splendid realisations of the early city.

The pictures provide an additional narrative. However, because a number of old photographs of Lincoln already exist, I have generally resisted reproducing pictures which can be found elsewhere but have chosen instead to use photographs of sites and structures as they appear now, in the hope that the reader will find it easier to recognise them in their present form. Many of these photographs have been taken by me, and I am indebted to Sue Latham of IRIS Photography and Video Productions of Sheffield and Chris Burnell of Wallingford for painstakingly turning my colour transparencies into black and white prints. I am also grateful to Chris, Keith and Kristian Beckwith for the tolerance with which they responded to my repeated requests to get a shot of a building or feature which I had overlooked. They have contributed numerous photographs. Many down the years have lent me old postcards and other pictures; as it is impossible to acknowledge them individually I hope that they will take pleasure from seeing their contribution here.

The place to begin is on the hill-brow, just below the Castle ramparts, and to look out south, across the valley of the Witham, to where the limestone scarp is picked up again on the other side of the river, swinging round through Northamptonshire and on into Oxfordshire and Gloucestershire to become the Cotswolds. Far beyond this, or so it is said, it re-emerges in France as the mountains of the Jura. Alternatively take your stand on the opposite side, looking north from Canwick Hill to the bulk of the Cathedral on its bluff on the other side of the valley. There are more dramatic gorges, but none speaks more clearly of its strategic possibilities than this broad gap, cut by the River Witham through the limestone scarp.

ABOVE: Lincoln from the west. The steepness of the scarp, variously referred to as The Edge, The Cliff, and, south of Lincoln, as The Heath, is here masked by housing development. BELOW: This painting in the City and County Museum, Lincoln, shows the Iron Age settlement below the hill as it might have been. LEFT: The shield was possibly a votive offering, cast into the River Witham at Lincoln.

12

Outpost of Empire

If we stood, 2,000 years ago, on the steep limestone hill where the Cathedral now stands, we would have looked out across a wide expanse of marshy fen (of which traces remain, albeit much domesticated, in the shape of the Brayford Pool and Hartsholme Lake). These wetlands extended as far as the eye could see, broken only by the line of the limestone scarp running north and south and interrupted by the gap cut by the river over the centuries. Immediately below us, much wider than its twentieth century canalised descendant, flowed the River Witham. Early human activity among these wetlands is attested by a mould used in making bronze axeheads from Washingborough, just across the valley, and a dug-out punt, dated to 850 BC, found at Fiskerton a little down-river from Lincoln.

The iron-using culture which appeared c500 BC, in the country around what was to become Lincoln, was richly developed. We must forget all about the county boundaries which much later divided the East Midlands. The Iron Age culture in this region belonged to a tribe, or federation of tribes, called the Coritani (or Coritavi), whose territories lay across the East Midlands. Its tribal capital was *Ratae Coritani* (Leicester). About the time of Julius Caesar's invasion the Coritani had begun to issue gold and silver coins, examples of which are displayed in the City and County Museum in Lincoln. One bears a horse on one side and a wild boar on the other. The wild boar also decorated the Witham Shield, one of the finest examples of Iron Age metalwork ever found, brought up from the bed of the Witham near Lincoln in 1826 and now on show in the British Museum. Another fine piece of Iron Age metalwork from the Witham on display in the Lincoln Museum is a sword and engraved bronze scabbard. These artefacts point to a highly developed society led by a rich warrior aristocracy.

Nevertheless, apart from these possibly religious offerings, the only other local evidence of human activity, before the Roman invasion of AD 43, are fragments of Iron Age pottery and remains of a round hut. These suggest a settlement existed on one of the gravel islands rising above the wet fen levels, along the margin of the Brayford Pool at the foot of the hill. The first element of the Roman name *Lindum* may share a root with the Welsh 'llyn', a lake, referring to this waterside settlement (for which the name 'Lindon' has been suggested). Other pottery of the first century of the Christian era has come from pits on the limestone edge, just north of the later city.

In AD 43 four legions of the Roman army invaded Britain. After pushing across the Thames into Essex, the legions fanned out in a three-pronged advance. The northern advance was undertaken by the Ninth (IX) Hispana, numbering over 5,000 men, originally raised in Spain. Its commanding officer, Aulus Plautius, was appointed overall c-in-c. The IX advanced along the line of the later Ermine Street, possibly building a road as it went, swinging west to skirt the marshy ground of Cambridgeshire and south Lincolnshire, then following a native trackway along the edge of the limestone scarp which rose above the wooded countryside of Kesteven (*Kest-* as the Welsh, 'coed', a wood; *-even*, possibly fen).

13

Forward units probably reached Lincoln before AD 50, and made camp about two kilometres south of the city, close to where excavation has revealed a military cemetery in use before then. This remained the IX Legion's base for ten years, which may explain why the military road, the Fosse Way, meets the Ermine Street near this point and not nearer the later legionary base. Part of the IX stayed on the Nene near modern Peterborough.

The base on top of the limestone scarp at *Lindum* seems to have been constructed ten years later, possibly as a result of the rebellion of Boudicca, Queen of the Iceni, whose tribal territories are now represented by modern East Anglia. When the tribal uprising began in AD 61 the commander of the IX Hispana at *Lindum* was Quintus Petillius Cerialus. He led a column to the relief of the new *colonia* for retired soldiers at *Camulodunum* (Colchester) which the Iceni had destroyed. However, the Iceni turned on the IX, annihilating it and pursued the survivors to the very gates of its base at *Lindum*.

2,000 troops from the Rhineland were required to bring the IX back up to strength. The new fortress on the stronger site 200 feet above sea-level was playing-card shaped, like all legionary bases. The first defences consisted of an earth and stone rampart eleven feet wide and seven feet high, faced with a wooden palisade or revetment topped by two-storey timber interval towers, and with a V-shaped ditch five yards wide and six feet deep in the solid limestone rock. A sentry walk ran round the top of the rampart.

At the centre of the foot stood the *principia* building of the legionary base, combining *basilica* (or aisled hall), chapel, and regimental offices. It was a timber building 65 metres by 60 metres, fronting onto the *via principalis* or main street (followed roughly by the modern Bailgate). This means that the fortress looked east (*not* north). Other streets, known or assumed, were the *via sagularis* which extended behind the entire circuit of the ramparts and the *via praetoria* crossing the *via principalis* east-west. The *via principalis* and *via praetoria* connected the gates which pierced the four sides of the playing card. Evidently, the main gate was not on the north (the Newport Arch) but the principal entrance into the upper walled area was by the Eastgate. This was a timber gateway, with two gate towers.

By the end of Nero's reign (54–68) there were military buildings on both banks of the River Witham. On the north bank the natives were probably compulsorily resettled in *canabae* (stalls or shops) since the land was required for installations supplying the garrison. The southern slope of the hill below the fortress developed as an area of shops, taverns, and other services.

The actual size of the garrison is uncertain. Only small sections of the barrack blocks on the forty acre legionary base have so far been excavated. Each block would have held two centuries, each of eighty men with its centurion and NCOs. One estimate suggests 250 men per acre. Part of the legion, perhaps a cohort (six centuries) in strength, may have been away on patrol, some garrisoning a forward post at Newton-on-Trent, covering the River Trent which formed the Northern frontier or *limes* of the Roman Empire, others guarding forts at Brough (*Crococalana*), Stoke (*Ad Pontem*), and Broxtowe (*Margidunum*), and all the way along the Fosse Way. This military road ran behind this natural frontier, linking *Lindum* with the western end of the newly-won Province. Other forts guarded the route of the Ermine Street south from *Lindum*.

The origins of some of the men in *Lindum* are known from their tombstones — Lucius Sempronius Flavinus from Spain or Gaius Sanfeius of the Fabian tribe, born at Heraclea in Macedonia, who died aged forty after 22 years' service. Another was Babudius Severus, centurion of the IX. Lost or discarded kit found by the archaeologists includes pieces of the body armour (*lorica segmenta*) worn by the legionaries, the support of a helmet crest, bits of ornamented scabbards, an axe sheath, and a ballista bolt. Each century followed its *signifer* or standard bearer, an animal skin covering his armour. Gaius Valerius was *signifer* in the century of Hospes of the IX. His tombstone, set up according to his will, tells us that he was 35 and had served 14 years.

Thus, for nearly two decades, *Lindum* was the northern-most point of the frontier of Rome. In the early seventies, however, the IX began to push forward across the Humber into Brigantian territory to deal with more unrest among the tribes and by AD 78 the Legion had been moved north to a new base at *Eboracum* (York), leaving a garrison of the II Adiutrix, marines from the Adriatic, in charge of *Lindum*. These troops were posted to Chester in AD 79 as part of the conquest of the west of Britain. What happened next is not certain. Possibly a small detachment was left to dismantle the base.

However, a stone tablet set up at Mainz by a citizen of *Lindum* in the reign of Domitian (81–96) shows that by AD 90 the town had become one of three in Britain to have *colonia* status (the others were at Colchester and Gloucester) and would henceforward be known as *Lindum Colonia*. This meant it would become the permanent home of time-expired legionaries, veterans of 25 years' service and their families and, as such, would provide a model of Roman urban life for the native population.

The newly-designated *Colonia* probably followed the street grid of the legionary fortress. The bath building in the north-east quarter of the uphill enclosure may well have been of legionary origin. The streets were resurfaced and new sewers laid. By the end of the first century an ambitious programme of public works was in hand. The fine paving, the bases upon which statues formerly stood, and the semi-circular apse uncovered in excavation suggest the legionary *principia* became a civic centre. Early in the reign of Hadrian (117–38) this area was radically redeveloped to create an impressive *forum* and *basilica* aligned north-south (as opposed to the east-west alignment of the legionary *principia*), bespeaking a magnificent scale of living. Although the centres of most other Roman British towns reveal their military origins, the forum of *Lindum Colonia* shows a continental influence, with a row of nineteen columns on the front (marked today by setts in the road along Bailgate: the bases of some columns survive in the cellars of houses here). At the sime time a new street was laid, north of the Mint Wall which marks the northern side of the *forum* complex. Most public buildings seem to have been located in the northern half of the uphill enclosure, while tessellated pavements uncovered in the southern half may have belonged to private domestic dwellings.

The administration of the *Colonia* was in the hands of the *decuriones*, a council (the *ordo*) of one hundred citizens, probably old soldiers, originally elected but later holding office for life. From the *decuriones* two magistrates, the *duumviri*, were chosen. The *basilica* building in the uphill part of the city probably housed the *Colonia* government, which also exercised control over the surrounding tribal area. The revenues of the *Colonia* came from rents on land allocated to the city, shops let to tenants, corn rents, and charges levied on traffic using the roads. Tombstones commemorate local dignitaries like the town councillor Aurelius Senecio, C. Antistius Frontinus, treasurer of the burial club, and Marcus Aurelius Lunaris, *sevir augustalis*, or priest of the important cult of Emperor worship at both *Lindum* and *Eboracum* (York).

As uphill, the street plan of the downhill area formed a grid, dividing the town into building blocks or *insulae*. Here several well-built private dwellings have been uncovered, equipped with hypocausts and standing in plots of land, together with more public buildings including more baths, a fountain, and a shrine. Unfortunately, however, terracing in the post-Roman period has destroyed much of the archaeological evidence on the hillside. Excavations at Michaelgate suggest that a stair, consisting of a series of steps constructed of limestone blocks set into the natural clay, led up the steep hill to the upper Roman town. Horses and wheeled vehicles would have been unable to use this stair and must have entered the upper part of the city from the east or north. Such a stair is unique among Roman cities north of the Alps.

The defences of *Lindum Colonia* were complex. Unusually, the legionary fortress was revetted with timber, perhaps because local turf proved inadequate. In the reign of Hadrian stone walls were built in front of the timber defences. As construction proceeded, the timbers of the legionary palisade were removed and the earth rampart was allowed to slip forward as a backing for the wall. The wooden gates were replaced by stone ones. Of the Newport Gate, only the south face survives but, in its complete state, this gate was 24 feet deep north-south with towers on either side. The gate had a single central arch for wheeled traffic 23 feet high and 16 feet wide, made of 26 wedged-shaped stones but without a keystone. There were arches for pedestrians on either side of the central roadway, each 15 feet high and seven feet wide. The main gate was the East Gate, with double arches for vehicles and two semi-circular bastions. Only the northern base of this gate is exposed today. The West Gate of the uphill enclosure was buried under the rampart of the Norman castle. Wall and ramparts were later further strengthened, sometimes at the expense of monuments and tombs, to a height of about seven metres, and the ditch was widened, so that by the fourth century the whole defensive barrier was over 100 yards across. The earliest fortifications around the lower city were not built until the late second century.

The excavation of several merchants' houses on the site of St Mark's Church shows that the Ermine Street was built up for at least a kilometre south of the lower walled city. Together with a farm and cemeteries north of the uphill walled area, this formed an urban zone three kilometres long and one and a half wide, and holding about 5,000 inhabitants. Inscriptions on tombstones show that people had come to *Lindum Colonia* from all over the Roman world — Gaul, Greece, Spain, Hungary, and Macedonia. From 212 all had Roman citizenship. The water supply to the *Colonia* on its 200 foot limestone cliff was along a pipeline carried on an aqueduct from springs to the north-east. It has been estimated that a double-action pump such as the Romans might have used could have lifted water ten feet, and delivered ten gallons a minute into the reservoir found just inside the north wall, which would require 16 hours' pumping to deliver a gallon per person per day.

Beyond the *Colonia* lay the land granted to the retired veterans, possibly still discernible in the geometrical parish boundaries of the villages bounding the Ermine Street north of Lincoln. The *Colonia* was connected to its hinterland by roads traced still by the Ermine Street, Fosse Way, and Tillbridge Lane, and by various minor roads, some of which can still be followed. In the *Colonia* the Ermine Street was paved with six inch-thick stone blocks, five or six inches square. It was carried over the marshy land on either side of the Witham by a 13 foot-high causeway. Likewise, the Fosse Way was carried on piles 12 feet high. North of the city the Ermine Street was laid on an *agger* (embankment) 41 feet wide. Besides the road system, there were waterways. The Car Dyke, possibly dug in Hadrian's reign, carried barges 56 miles from the Nene, along the Witham, up to *Lindum* while the Fosse Dyke completed the canal system from the Brayford Pool to the River Trent eleven miles away. The Brayford waterfront was probably important but so far little is known about it. Apart from local trade, food, salt from the coast, and pottery, the commercial life of the *Colonia* touched all corners of the Roman Empire — wine from Bordeaux, amphorae of oil or fruit from Spain, marble from Greece, Italy, and Asia Minor, glass from Alexandria and Germany, Samian Pottery from the Rhineland and France.

After the third century some streets began to decay. Others, however, remained in use for another hundred years. Indeed, the end of the fourth century saw the construction of a number of important new buildings, including a Christian church. Under Diocletian (284–305), *Lindum Colonia* was elevated to be the capital of *Flavia Caesariensis*, one of the four provinces into which Britain was now divided. The fortifications were refurbished on a massive scale. In the mid-4th century the west gate of the downhill town was reconstructed on monumental proportions, in keeping with its new dignity, incorporating stone from other buildings. At the same time there is evidence of deliberate land reclamation along the Witham outside the city wall. There are also indications of a garrison presence once more. Hence, the picture of *Lindum*, on the eve of the withdrawal of Roman power, is one of prosperity and confidence.

ABOVE LEFT: The tombstone of the standard-bearer of a unit of the IX at Lincoln. RIGHT: The Newport Arch or north gate in Hadrian's walls around the upper city. A pedestrian way has now been inserted to the left of the arch.

BELOW LEFT: The Mint Wall which formed part of the Roman forum. RIGHT: The remains of the south gate of the upper city by the Leopard Tavern, a print of 1788.

ABOVE: An impression of the forum-basilica, the Roman civic centre.
LEFT: The base of the north turret of the east gate, the principal entrance
to the uphill town. RIGHT: A charioteer's tombstone; the whereabouts of
the Roman racecourse is not known.

ABOVE: Base of the great west gate of the lower city, built in the last Roman century, excavated in 1971. LEFT: Reconstruction of the west gate of the lower city. It incorporates fragments of a former temple, disused perhaps when Christianity became the official religion of the Empire. RIGHT: Roman *carbatina*, a slipper made from a single piece of leather; from the Waterside North site.

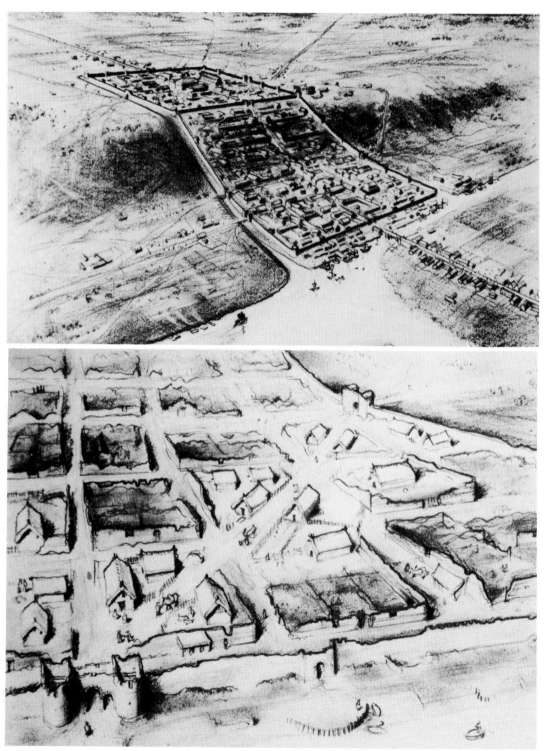

ABOVE: Impression of the Roman city from the south-west. BELOW: An impression of the lower city before the Conquest. Silver Street now cuts diagonally through the Roman street grid.

Free Under God

In the mid-4th century, possibly contemporary with the strengthening of *Lindum*'s defences, steps were taken to defend the coastline against sea-borne attacks by raiders from the region now called the Netherlands, North Germany, and Denmark. A line of coastal forts and two fleets were established to guard the shore from the Solent to the Humber. This security endured no more than a hundred years. By the mid-5th century, 400 years of Roman presence in *Lindum Colonia* were at an end and the Imperial government left the local population to fend for itself.

The archaeological evidence suggests a period of settlement near Roman garrison towns, by early migrants from northern Europe, during the last stages of Roman administration. These migrations were more numerous by the time the Romans pulled out in 450. The native population reverted to tribal loyalties. Contrary to earlier belief, *Lindum* did not go up in a holocaust. A small settlement managed to survive inside the Roman walls during the fifth and sixth centuries, although the lower city seems to have been deserted. Early in this confused period, the former Roman *colonia* of *Lindum* became the capital of a small kingdom, bounded by the Humber, Witham, Trent, and the sea. This small, politically insignificant kingdom continued the name *Lindum* in its title Lindsey (*-ey* meaning island, a reference to the water-girt kingdom). One of the earliest kings in the royal line of this little kingdom bore a British name.

Writing in 731, in his *History of the English Church and People*, the Venerable Bede referred to Blecca, the *Praefectus* of the city in 628, which might indicate some survival of Roman civic offices. More probably Blecca was a sub-king or official of the Northumbrian high king whose client kingdom Lindsey was. The modern name of Lincoln is a further sign of continuity, incorporating elements of the Roman title *Lindum Colonia*. Nevertheless, as buildings fell into ruin, it was not long before new lanes were made across Roman property boundaries and street alignments, finding the short cuts to the main gates, and the Roman street plan began to disintegrate.

Bede was writing about what he believed was the earliest Christian mission to Lincoln, about a generation after St Augustine reached Kent in 595. However, Bede may not have realised that, barely a decade after the death of St Alban, during Emperor Diocletian's persecution of Christians between 303–5, and only one year after Constantine sanctioned Christianity, Adelfius, Bishop of Lincoln, was present at a Council of the Church at Arles in Gaul. This suggests that there was, in Roman Lincoln in the early fourth century, a Christian church — a community much like the churches in Asia Minor to whom St Paul addressed his epistles. The Bishop would have presided over this early Christian community or parish, assisted by priests and deacons. Parish, in this case, did not refer to a definite geographical area. The rest is surmise. Could Bishop Adelfius have been the head of a large territorial diocese? The term 'diocese', referring to the entire area, city and country, under a bishop's authority, was not adopted from the Roman Imperial administration until the next century. By the end of the fifth century, a diocesan structure within the framework of the tribal kingdoms probably existed, led by vigorous missionary bishops. As the capital of a province of fourth century Britain, Lincoln might well have become the seat of a diocesan bishop. In token of this, a piece from the hoard of fourth century church silver, found at Water Newton on the site of the Roman town of *Durobrivae* near Peterborough, can be seen in the Treasury of Lincoln Cathedral. The cups, spoons, and half-pagan votive offerings of the Water Newton treasure are among the earliest objects associated with Christian worship in the world and probably belonged to a large church, which it is tempting to imagine lay within the diocese of a bishop at *Lindon*.

Either way, the outlines of a fourth century church building have been located in uphill Lincoln, in the centre of the *forum* itself. This city-centre church may well have served as the *basilica* of the bishops of Roman Lincoln. Its continuing importance is indicated by the use of the site for Christian burials into the sixth century. There is therefore strong evidence of the presence of a Christian community in Lincoln *before* the conversion of *praefectus* Blecca which Bede described. This casts some doubt on Bede's assessment. It seems surprising that no memory remained then of Lincoln's place in the history of Christianity. Although the church on the *forum* had not been in use since the end of Roman Britain, the Christian burials there suggest it was still seen as consecrated ground in the next century. Less than a hundred years later, a new church was built on the site, on top of the *basilica* of the Roman bishops.

Perhaps Bede wished to give the credit for establishing Christianity in Lincoln to Paulinus, the emissary from the Roman pope. Less than a generation after Paulinus's mission to Lincoln, the claims of the Roman Church to ecclesiastical jurisdiction over England had prevailed over the native Celtic Church, bringing the Church in England into line with mainstream orthodoxy. For Bede the hero of Catholic Christianity in Lincoln could only be St Paulinus. The city prefect Blecca was the first Christian. Paulinus built the 'first' church, described by Bede as of remarkable workmanship.

The seventh century building which obliterated the traces above ground of the fourth century church, and which tradition claims was the one built by St Paulinus in 628, was extraordinary. Built in stone, with a large apsidal east end divided by a stone screen from the nave, on the model of *basilicas* in Rome familiar to Paulinus, it stood on the site of the later medieval church of St Paul-in-the-Bail, and was twenty-one metres in length. The unusual dedication of the later church to St Paul, may in fact have originated with this second church on the site, proclaiming that this was when Lincoln's Christians were baptised into the true Catholic faith by Paulinus and relegating Bishop Adelfius and his parish to limbo.

There is one other puzzle concerning this seventh century church. Where the altar would have stood a grave was found, empty save for a hanging bowl of the seventh century, elaborately decorated and inlaid with enamels and millefiori work. Such bowls have previously been found in pagan burials but this is the first discovered in an unambiguously Christian context. Probably the pagan custom of furnishing objects to accompany the departed to the next world was continued into the Christian era (as in the Sutton Hoo burial ship), suggesting a precarious Christian hold on the hearts and minds of Anglian Lincoln. The position of the grave shows that it was intended for an important person, perhaps of Royal rank, maybe the lay founder of the church or its benefactor. The absence of a body is strange. Perhaps it was translated to another, more important, church or — like the East Anglian king whose burial ship was laid beneath the mounds of Sutton Hoo at the same time — sent forth upon the waters.

It was the Danish Vikings who shaped the medieval and, to some extent, the modern city of Lincoln. From 871 they gave an enormous impetus to urban development. The suburb of Wigford may take its name from the Viking period. By the early tenth century Lincoln had already regained its status as a major town. Coins and pottery show that the settled area had expanded considerably before 900. Excavations on Flaxengate and Grantham Street have shown that two streets thought part of the Roman grid pattern were really new ones laid out in the Viking period.

Flaxengate (formerly *Haraldstigh*) existed by 880 and Grantham Street (or *Brancegate*) was laid out by the mid-eleventh century). As on the famous Coppergate site at York (*Jorvik*), so too on the Flaxengate site, small-scale industrial processes were carried on in timber buildings (which were periodically demolished and rebuilt). The finished products included glass rings, beads, jet and copper objects, and textiles. Coins from York, Chester, and Hereford, pottery from north-west Europe, the Near East, and even China, products from the Baltic, especially jewellery from Scandinavia, show that Lincoln's trading links extended as far and wide in the Viking period as they had done under Rome. It is possible that a mint was working in Lincoln by 921.

The buildings on the Flaxengate site were systematically cleared roughly every generation, making thirteen phases of building from 870 to 1200. Further evidence of Lincoln's prosperity in the Viking period has been brought to light from excavation at Michaelgate, which has revealed the earliest known post-Roman stone building. Timber and stone buildings succeeded one another on this site from the tenth to the twelfth century, housing a malting kiln, metal-working, and various pits, including two crude mortar mixers. Meanwhile land along the Witham was systematically reclaimed to form a 'hard', extending the waterfront southwards.

Not surprisingly, the Vikings had a 'garrison' in Lincoln. It was one of the so-called 'Five Boroughs' of the Danelaw, a centre from which Viking power was exercised over the surrounding 'shire' (as in 'to shear', cut or divide) of Lindsey from behind the old Roman walls. Lindsey was divided into 'Ridings', from an Old Danish word meaning 'a third'. Within these Ridings were other divisions called 'wapentakes' (weapon-raisings), centred on a meeting place. Also of Danish origin were the hereditary lawmen of Lincoln, originally twelve in number, whose duty was to see that the laws and customs of this important town were safeguarded. These custodians and expounders of the law were still functioning at the time of Domesday (1086) and may have survived as the twelve aldermen who appear as close companions of the Mayor in the later middle ages.

What the Normans found was a flourishing community. Much of the area of the former Roman city was again built up and the street system was largely in being by 1066. It recovered some of the prominence it had in Roman times. By 1086 Lincoln probably ranked as the third city in England, equal with Winchester and Norwich and only surpassed by York and London. Coins are evidence of this prosperity. From the time of King Edgar's reform of the coinage in 973 Lincoln became one of the four or five most important mints. Coins found here suggest that Lincoln's trade with the rest of England was greater than that of York and that, in terms of coins carried over the North Sea to the Baltic, Lincoln was second only to London. Indeed, by the mid-eleventh century, the mint may have ranked second in the land.

Lincoln was a city of freemen — either the sons of freemen, or persons who had gained their freedom by living for a year and a day in Lincoln, or persons who paid the king's 'land-gable' or land tax to the Royal Bailiff. In many cases the freemen represented another legacy of Danish Lincoln, being descendants of those pre-Conquest Viking citizens who peopled the houses and workshops on Flaxengate and from whom the lawmen mentioned in Domesday were chosen. These freemen were not passive subjects of a feudal system. They carried a heavy responsibility for the city's security and for ensuring that it functioned effectively. Thus every freeman undertook to repair the walls or paid 'murage' to hire masons to do the work. After the castle was built, those living in the Bail paid for the hire of knights to do castle guard. All freemen attended the weekly meetings of the 'burwarmot', or borough court, at the mootstone in the churchyard of St Peter-ad-Placita (-at-Pleas) on the east side of Mikelgate (the main street above the Stonebow). This dealt with the day-to-day management of life under the supervision of the King's Bailiff. The 'burwarmot' was the equivalent of the rural manor court. Among other matters it was concerned with the tenure of property. Twenty-four inhabitants were chosen to form a council, which elected the officers (coroners, constables, auditors) and maintained jurisdiction through the 'burwarmot'.

Of the twenty-four, half were empowered as justices. The 'burwarmot' decided each freeman's share of the money due to the King. Under the Old English kings this had been twenty pounds; under the Norman kings it became one hundred pounds per man, a reflection no doubt of Lincoln's growing prosperity.

The new streets and houses and associated industrial activity of the tenth-twelfth centuries are indicative of a vigorous urban community. Estimates of population in 1086 put it between five and eight thousand. It would have taken a thousand head of cattle, 1,400 sheep, and 800 pigs to supply a year's meat for this number, necessitating for the sheep alone at least 10,000 acres of grazing, not to speak of the grain requirements of the city. The people who occupied the Flaxengate houses in the tenth and eleventh centuries also kept pets. Dogs were held in high esteem. The larger boned were doubtless guard dogs but smaller boned dogs were probably pets. Skeletal remains of cats were more numerous in the eleventh century but most died within eighteen months. Horse bones are uncommon, suggesting they were not important in this quarter.

The Bishop of Lincoln celebrates the eucharist in the excavations of St Paulinus's church on the Feast of St Paulinus, 10 October 1978.

LEFT: The Lincoln Hanging Bowl, in situ in the empty tomb, and RIGHT:
after restoration. BELOW: The Flaxengate excavations which revealed for
the first time how prosperous Danish Lincoln was.

LEFT: Silver penny of Cnut, dating between 1024–30, from the Lawn Hospital site. RIGHT: The Greenstone Steps, leading into the upper city, from an Old Danish word meaning stair. BELOW: St Mary's Stow-by-Lincoln, one of the largest pre-Conquest churches north of the Alps, long believed to be the mother church of Lindsey but built as a cell of the Abbey of Eynsham in Oxfordshire.

Power Politics

It is hardly surprising that the first Norman King should make the third city of his realm the site of both a castle and a cathedral church. The conditions in the years following 1066 demanded garrisons (made up of armed, mounted retainers called knights) at strategic points to secure the, as yet fragile, Norman Conquest from its internal and external enemies. Castles provide an index of Norman control. Lincoln's was one of several constructed by William in 1067–70. The problem in the East Midlands was a Danish fleet of about 240 longships which, after cruising along the east coast, made a landing on the Humber shore in 1069. The invaders were welcomed by local people, many of whom (in some districts, such as the Lincolnshire Wolds, perhaps 75 per cent) were of Danish descent. Together the invaders and the Lincolnshire and Yorkshire rebels moved on York, wiping out its Norman garrison. King William led his army swiftly northward, dealt with rebels in Staffordshire, then turned to deal with Yorkshire, where his troops laid waste the countryside round York.

Most of the Roman walls of Lincoln still stood. As one of the Five Boroughs of the Danelaw, the city was well-fortified. However, few had ever seen anything like the castle which William raised at Lincoln in 1068. Although some of Edward the Confessor's Norman favourites had built themselves castles in the south and English visitors to Normandy had brought back accounts of castles there, the ones which William now erected in England were innovations. The castle brought the Conquest and the feudal system forcibly to Lincoln.

The site selected was, not surprisingly, the same steep-faced promontory which the Romans had chosen one thousand years ago. Roman masonry has recently been found beneath the Norman west gate. Whereas the great base for the 5,000 men of the IX Hispana had covered forty acres, the new Norman Castle occupied only thirteen and a half. Nevertheless, 166 houses had to be demolished, displacing at least 800 inhabitants or perhaps a tenth of the population. By comparison, Norwich only lost 98 houses for its castle; at Canterbury 32 were pulled down. Lincoln was obviously one of the largest. It was of the type known as 'motte and bailey', consisting of a mound (the 'motte') and enclosed yard (the 'bailey'). At Lincoln the bailey, or castle yard, was six and a quarter acres, more than twice the normal area. The bailey was surrounded by earthen banks 20 to 30 feet high and 50 to 80 yards wide, with a ditch on the west, north, and east. The motte was 40 feet high and 100 feet in diameter at the summit and was surmounted by a wooden tower or keep. From the castle, watch could be kept over the town below and across the countryside, west and south in the direction of the new Royal castle at Nottingham and the baronial castles at Belvoir and Laxton. In due course the Bishops of Lincoln would also have a castle at Newark-on-Trent.

The original timber defences on top of the earthen ramparts were probably replaced by stone walls between forty and fifty years later, by which time the soil was compacted enough to carry them. On the other hand the east and west gates may have had stone foundations from at least 1086. Some time before 1136, the stone keep called the Lucy Tower, named after the Countess

Lucy de Taillebois, wife of the Sheriff of Lincoln, replaced the wooden tower on top of the motte. Lincoln Castle was a Royal castle, under the command of a constable, and garrisoned by knights provided by powerful local barons, such as the Bishops of Lincoln. The Constableship of Lincoln Castle was held by the descendants of Colsuen, the English constable under William I. In 1115 Robert de la Haye inherited the role.

Seventy years after it was built, Lincoln Castle fell into the hands of the Earl of Chester, Ranulf 'les Gernons' (moustaches), son of Countess Lucy de Taillebois. His lands amounted to almost a third of the kingdom and included large estates in Lincolnshire. His intention was to link his scattered possessions by a series of strongholds. His half-brother, Lucy's son William de Roumare, had also inherited large Lincolnshire estates and claimed the Constableship of Lincoln Castle. In 1140, while their wives paid a social call on the Constable's wife, the two brothers and their men-at-arms managed to get inside the Castle and seized the Lucy Tower.

They strengthened it and organised reinforcements, consisting of retainers from Cheshire, Welsh levies and the forces of Ranulf's father-in-law, the Earl of Gloucester. However, before these arrived, the burgesses of Lincoln appealed to King Stephen. When the Welsh under Prince Cadwallader, the Earl of Gloucester's army and the Earl of Chester's men reached Lincoln on the Feast of the Purification, Candlemas, 2 February 1141, they found the King besieging the Castle, using the parapets and embrasures of the cathedral to position bowmen and siege weapons. Although the Witham was in flood, it being 'February fill-dyke', the Earls got across, possibly at Boultham, crossed the Foss Dyke west of the Brayford, and approached from the Carholme and the West Common onto level ground north-west of the Castle.

Meanwhile, the King was at Mass in the Cathedral. As he handed his offering of a wax candle to the Bishop he dropped it and it broke. The chain holding the pyx above the High Altar snapped and the Blessed Sacrament fell to the floor. This was regarded as a warning against daring to begin his attack during the Twelve Days of Christmas. To add to his problems, the King's voice was too weak to be heard by his army and his speech before battle had to be delivered by Baldwin Fitz-Gilbert, Lord of Clare. Nevertheless, the King fought as befitted the grandson of William the Conqueror, wielding a great Norse two-edged axe given him by a citizen of Lincoln. 'The battle was seen to rage horribly . . . helmets and swords gleamed as they clashed, and the dreadful noise re-echoed from the hills and walls of the city'. Eventually the King was brought down by a stone from behind. The rest of his army was driven from the field and he was taken prisoner. This became known as the 'Joust of Lincoln'.

Lincoln Castle was besieged twice more during Stephen's reign. In 1146 he took Ranulf prisoner and compelled him to surrender all his castles. Stephen kept the Christmas Feast at Lincoln and wore his crown in defiance of an old saying that

> 'The first crowned head that enters Lincoln's walls
> His reign proves stormy and his kingdom falls'.

As soon as Stephen left Lincoln, Ranulf attacked again, but had to withdraw. In 1149 Stephen needed Ranulf's support against Henry of Anjou, Matilda's son. Accordingly he granted Lincoln Castle and city to the Earl of Chester and allowed him to fortify a tower. This probably refers to the motte and Observatory Tower in the south-east corner of the Castle, which dates from that period. Henry became King on Stephen's death in 1154 and Lincoln Castle was surrendered to him. Throughout the struggle between Ranulf and Stephen, the de la Hayes had held the constableship. From 1188 it was held jointly by Nicholaa, daughter of Richard de la Haye, and her husband, Gerard de Camville.

Almost thirty years later, Nicholaa was still Constable when the Castle again came under attack during the war between King John and the barons; she held it against the rebel barons and their French allies, until she was relieved by the Royal army. Led by William the Marshal it approached Lincoln from Torksey and Stow. Part of the King's force was admitted *via* the postern gate and bombarded the besieging rebels from the walls, while the rest fought its way into the city by the Newport Arch. Once in the Bail the Royal force reunited, routing the French army. This time the battle raged through the town as the rebels fell back, fighting hand-to-hand down the High Street, until their retreat was cut off by the Great Bargate, closed against them. Swords and coats of mail found in the Witham when it was deepened in 1826 belonged to French soldiers driven into the river and drowned. People called this battle the 'Fair of Lincoln'. After, city and Cathedral were put to the sack for supporting the rebel cause. Nicholaa continued to hold the constableship until 1226, dying in 1230.

After the 'Fair of Lincoln' the Castle needed extensive repairs and £500 was spent between 1218 and 1224 to bring the defences up-to-date. In 1224 twenty pounds was spent on repairs to the Lucy Tower and 'the eastern gate facing the Minster and in making a barbican to protect it'. This formed two high, battlemented side walls, extending in front of the innermost gateway and a narrow outer gate flanked by twin towers opening onto the Bail. Any attackers penetrating this outer gate would be trapped in the confined space between the barbican walls and the inner gate, while the defenders rained projectiles and the proverbial boiling oil on their heads.

During this same period the tower known as Cobb Hall was constructed. Horseshoe or D-shaped in plan, it is typical of the towers of new castles such as those built in Wales in the thirteenth century. In 1831 two hundred stone balls thought to be ammunition for a catapult were found in a recess in the tower. From a firing platform on its top these could have been directed onto attackers approaching the north and east sides. Originally Cobb Hall had a third storey, probably containing a small suite of rooms. For much of its history the two lower stages of the tower were used as dungeons. However, no further military action was seen until 1644 and by 1327 towers, walls, the great hall and other quarters were in ruins and beyond repair. Excavation has shown that the west gate went out of use about the same time.

Sections of the castle ditch were rented to merchants, who set up market stalls. The constable held his own court baron for Castle tenants in the Bail and kept the assay of weights and measures for the city. Eventually the hereditary constableship descended to the Earldom of Lincoln and thence passed by marriage to the Earls of Lancaster, thus in due course becoming Duchy of Lancaster property, administered by the Crown. The Castle continued to function as the location of the county courts and the county gaol. In 1826 the assize court, where the Crown Court is still held, was built. Since 1831, when the county magistrates bought the Castle, it has also housed the county magistrates' courts. In 1878 the gaol was transferred to a new building on Greetham Road, on the east side of the city.

Kings and their courts were peripatetic. The seat of government was wherever the King happened to be in his realm. Thus on 26 September 1300 Edward I summoned his parliament to meet him at Lincoln in 1301 and instructed the Sheriff to procure 800 quarters of wheat, 400 quarters of malt, 1,000 quarters of oats, 200 cows and oxen, 700 sheep, 160 pigs, and hay for 400 horses for one month. The quantity requisitioned for just one month, even when allowance is made for extravagance, would have fed the entire city for almost three times this period, implying that Lincoln's population was increased by over 3,500 people for the occasion. At this Parliament Edward I created his son Edward first Prince of Wales and then told the Pope that the Crown of England was independent of the See of Rome. Parliament also met in Lincoln twice in 1316, when every parish was required to furnish a man-at-arms for 60 days for the King's expedition into Scotland, and again in 1327, in the Chapter House of the Cathedral, presumably 'in the round', a shape which, if it had been kept instead of the two opposing sides in the choir stalls of St Stephen's Chapel, Westminster, might have inhibited development of the English oppositional political system. The burgesses of Lincoln were first summoned to send representatives to a parliament as early as 1265.

Edward I was again in Lincoln when his Queen, Eleanor of Castile, died from what was called a slow fever. On this occasion the King was meeting Parliament at the Royal hunting lodge at Clipstone in Nottinghamshire. The Queen was moved to Harby near Lincoln and on 18 October syrops were brought from Lincoln. The King was with her at Harby from 20 to 29 November, when she died. He came to Lincoln while the corpse was embalmed before its winter journey south, possibly leaving on 4 December. The Queen's body had rested at the Gilbertine Priory of St Catherine's on the southern outskirts of the city and the first of ten Eleanor Crosses marking where her body rested, was placed nearby on Swine Green, on the edge of the South Common. Destroyed in the year before Charles I was beheaded, two feet of the base survive in the Castle grounds. King Edward was at Casterton on 5 December, at Northampton on the 9th, and back in London on the 13th.

Relationships between Edward II and his baronial subjects were uneasy, partly because he raised money from Italian bankers such as Emery de Frescobaldi and partly because the barons disliked the influence which the King's favourites, such as Henry de Beaumont, exercised at Court. As security the King allowed Emery de Frescobaldi the income from the court of the knight's fee of Hungate in Lincoln. However, in 1311 the barons compelled him to get rid of both de Frescobaldi and de Beaumont. In spite of this, Edward II managed to give Emery's Lincoln estate to Henry de Beaumont's sister, to hold for her life and after to revert to Henry. The name Beaumont Fee for the area of streets between West Parade and Newland recalls this episode. The manor of Beaumont or Hungate was exempt from the jurisdiction of the city (having a separate Bailiff, who took precedence over the city Sheriffs), as also were Castle and Bail. So, too, was the Precinct of the Close around the Cathedral. These formed Liberties, free from outside authority. Those living there were not subject to dues levied by the city. Moreover, they were a refuge for those who wished to escape the jurisdiction of Mayor and Bailiffs.

In the Cathedral library is one of the exemplars of Magna Carta sent out to all parts of the realm after King John and his barons met at Runnymede on 15 June 1215. There was not one 'original' Charter as such but duplicates were made to be dispatched to the principal cities. Of these 'originals' four survive; the Lincoln one is still where it was sent in 1215. Its witnesses include Hugh of Lincoln, that is Bishop Hugh de Welles, St Hugh's successor. It was not the first charter of this kind. Indeed, its forerunners are the town charters which guaranteed the rights and privileges of urban corporations such as Lincoln. Nor were the provisions of Magna Carta, such as Clause 14, which seems to contain the seeds of the slogan 'no taxation without representation', without precedent. Magna Carta was a conservative document, intended by the barons to 'put the clock back', to resist the erosion of feudal customs going on since the time of John's father, Henry II. Nevertheless, it has come to be seen throughout the English-speaking world as the basis of such rights as trial by jury, Habeas Corpus, equality before the law, and freedom from arbitrary arrest. For that reason Lincoln's Magna Carta often travels the Atlantic to represent those rights in the 'Land of the Free'.

collocauit. ꝗſuleſ cū ſuiſ in duabuſ Aciebuſ equiſ pug
naturoſ inſtituit. Seo Admodū parue equeſtreſ acieſ ille
ꝛ paruerunt. Paucoſ enim ſecū fici ꝗ faccioſi ꝗſuleſ Ad
duxerant. Acieſ autem regaliſ maxima erat. uno tm̄ ſa
licet ipſiuſ regiſ inſignita uexillo. Tunc quia rex Stephꝰ
feſtiua carebat uoce: baldewino filio Gilleb magne nobili
catiſ uiro ꞇ milici foriſſimo ſermo exhortatoriꝰ ad uniuſu ecm
iniunctuſ eſt.

ABOVE: The outer bailey of the castle, looking west towards the east gate and the barbican. BELOW: The Battle of Lincoln, 1141. King Stephen, having lost his voice, has delegated the exhortation before the battle to Baldwin fitz Gilbert. RIGHT: The west gate and approach road revealed by excavation in 1987.

31

OPPOSITE ABOVE: The castle as it might have appeared about 1190. BELOW: This view of the easternmost of the two mounds or mottes shows the strong defensive position of the castle. ABOVE: The eastern motte and east gate from the inner bailey. CENTRE: This southward panorama along the battlements shows castle and cathedral in a close strategic relationship. BELOW: The castellated Observatory built by a Victorian prison governor on the eastern motte.

LEFT: Cobb Hall about 1250. RIGHT:
The east gate and barbican about 1240.
BELOW: The Lincoln Magna Carta.

Monument of Love Divine

Four years after the Castle was built that other pillar of eleventh century society, the Church, established its presence. Henceforth, the Church assumed a share in the task of Normanisation. The Cathedral was a more complex centre of power than the Castle because it represented both divine *and* temporal authority. In the year after the Conquest, Wulfwig, Bishop of Mid-Anglia and Lindsey, died. In his place King William appointed Remi (Remigius), almoner of the Abbey of Fecamp in Normandy, the first Norman to be made bishop after the Conquest. His see (seat or throne) was in the small Oxfordshire township of Dorchester-on-Thames, in the south-west corner of the diocese, many days away by horse nine centuries ago. Moreover Dorchester lay in Wessex, in the patrimony of the Old English Royal house, making it a potential rallying point for the disaffected.

At the synod at Windsor in 1072 an ancient law of the Church was reaffirmed, prohibiting the siting of episcopal sees in villages. Before Pope Alexander died in 1073 Remi got papal sanction, and the King's writ, to transfer the see to Lincoln. He is said to have bought land near the Castle which the King made free and quit of all customary dues. Some say that the new Norman church was built on the site of a pre-Conquest minster, also dedicated to the Blessed Virgin, referred to in the Domesday Survey. Certainly the term 'minster' is often used of the Cathedral Church and its precincts are locally called 'Minster Yard'. The construction of the new church, which was to house the Bishop's 'cathedra' or throne, was begun in 1075. By 1092 it was said to be perfect. Although there is no reference in the Domesday Book to the destruction of houses to make room for it, the Survey, carried out seven years before the Cathedral was finished, states that 74 houses were empty ('waste') outside the Castle boundary.

The new Church was placed in the south-east corner of the outer bailey of the Castle and hence was part of the defences. The position of the Cathedral had tactical implications, given the instability of the Kingdom in the years following the Conquest. It was vital that it should not be a weak point. Thus the Norman Bishops were not only spiritual leaders but also barons, under charge to provide 20 knights for the defence of the Castle, while the new Cathedral Church itself was constructed on the lines of a stronghold or keep. The thick walls of the massive Norman west front are honeycombed with passages and small chambers, lit by narrow slits, which could contain defenders in the event of attack.

Bishop Remi of Lincoln died on the day before his new Cathedral Church was to have been consecrated and this ceremony was delayed until after the appointment, in 1093, of the new Bishop, Robert Bloet. The Old English minster had had, perhaps, seven canons (*canon*, from the Latin for rule, hence priests living under a rule), some of whom may have been married. The constitution of the new Church was modelled on the Cathedrals of Rouen and Bayeux. This required 21 celibate canons in line with continental practice. This vastly increased establishment was supported by grants of land from the King to provide the prebends (literally, bread) of the canons. Besides the canons, the establishment consisted of the Precentor (in charge of the music),

35

Treasurer, Chancellor (in charge of the scriptorum and seals), and Dean, who ruled over all like the prior of a monastery, presiding over the canons assembled in Chapter in the Chapter House. The Bishop was as an abbot, the father-in-God of them all. Indeed, we are told that Bishop Hugh of Lincoln regularly ate with his canons (in the same way as an abbot would eat with his monks or a lord with his knights).

In addition to the existence of a Chapter House and cloisters, this analogy with a monastery is some help in coming to terms with the special character of the Cathedral Church of the Blessed Virgin Mary of Lincoln. It has never been a parish church although, after the church of St Mary Magdalene had been demolished for the extension of the Cathedral, the parishioners were permitted for a time to use the Morning Chapel, where the first mass of the morning was offered, in the north-west corner of the Cathedral. The Cathedral choir was like the choir of a monastic church, where the canons said or heard the daily offices (of which matins and evensong are still said or sung in the Cathedral every morning and evening). The Cathedral nave was, in the phrase of a former Subdean, Canon Cook 'a great vestibule to the Choir', used for the processions of the canons on High Days and Holy Days. Until 1790, when the nave was refloored, two parallel rows of 37 slabs marked the stations at which the priests stood, during the sprinklings of the altar before the screen with holy water every Sunday. Sermons were delivered by one of the canons to his fellows in choir. On certain festivals the Chancellor, or a priest appointed by him, preached to the people in the nave. Once, during the time of Robert Grosseteste (Bishop 1235–53) who had incurred the special hostility of the canons, the canon preaching a sermon inveighing against the Bishop cried out 'were we silent, the very stones would cry out for us', whereupon the central tower collapsed.

This event in 1239 was by no means the first occasion that the Cathedral had been damaged. Little more than 30 years after the first Norman Cathedral had been perfected, the tomb of its founder, Bishop Remi, was damaged by fire and his body was translated to its present resting place on the north side of the sanctuary before the high altar. Sixteen years later the Cathedral was again damaged during the Civil War between the Empress Matilda and King Stephen. After the Joust of Lincoln in 1141, the Cathedral seems to have been severely damaged by fire, perhaps during the sacking of the city when several churches were burned down. Accordingly the Bishop, Alexander, known as 'the Magnificent', carried out a restoration, introducing rich Romanesque ornament and also reducing its capability as a stronghold.

Little more than forty years later the splendid Romanesque Cathedral was seriously damaged again, possibly in an earthquake which split it from top to bottom. The Bishop to whom fell the task of rebuilding was one of the most remarkable churchmen of an age which produced Thomas à Becket and Bernard of Clairvaux, and would yet produce Francis of Assisi. History knows him as St Hugh of Lincoln but he was born Hugo, son of William 'sieur' (lord) of the castle of Avalon in Imperial Burgundy (now in the region of the Dauphiné in south-east France, near the ski resort of Val d'Isère) and Anne.

After Anne's death, father and son entered the order of the Austin Canons. At 19 Hugo was given charge of a small parish near the Carthusian Abbey of La Grande Chartreuse. He became a Carthusian monk. After Thomas à Becket was martyred Henry II endowed three abbeys, including a small Carthusian foundation at Witham in Somerset. At the King's request, Hugo of Avalon became Prior of Witham revitalizing the monastery, and in 1186 the King chose him as his Bishop of Lincoln. But Hugh, like Thomas à Becket, was opposed to Royal interference. He refused the King's nomination and insisted on a free election by the canons of Lincoln in their own chapter house. Even then he only accepted the See on the express command of the Prior of La Grande Chartreuse. Hugh was consecrated in Westminster Abbey on 21 September 1186 and enthroned in his Cathedral Church eight days later. He arrived in Lincoln with his monastic habit in his saddlebag. The former prior with charge over 30 monks in a little Somerset monastery now had 56 canons and a vast staff of masons, choristers, and doorkeepers, a great, if ruined, church, and a huge diocese containing over 1,900 parishes and a fifth of the population of England, eight palaces, and a personal retinue of thirty knights.

The fact that Hugh was able to take his seat on his throne implies the building was not a complete ruin. In any case, this was not his only problem. The diocese had been without a bishop for two years, following 20 years of instability. Hugh now threw himself into the role. Although Henry II had taken such a personal interest in his advancement, the King found his new Bishop obdurate in safeguarding the rights of God's Church. When the Royal Foresters abused some of Hugh's clergy, Hugh excommunicated them. He was summoned to Henry's palace at Woodstock (then in Lincoln diocese) where he found King and court in the Park. Hugh's greeting was met with silence. After he had made a space to sit, he waited for the King to speak. The King began to stitch a leather wrist strap. Hugh took his cue: 'You remind me of your cousins of Falaise'. The King burst out laughing, explaining to his entourage Hugh's reference to William the Conqueror, whose mother was a tanner's daughter.

Hugh loved children, visited the sick, especially lepers whom he bathed in his own chamber, as his mother had done, and buried the dead, especially the poor, often delaying official business so to do. Over 200 acts survive from his episcopacy, bearing witness to his efficiency and hard work. At that time the schools at Oxford were only just beginning and the schools of Lincoln were second only to those of the University of Paris. He gathered around him men of talent, such as his archdeacons, Gerald of Wales and Walter Map. Also in his household was a clever young deacon, Master Robert Grosseteste. Yet Hugh found time to return every year to Witham to live as a simple monk. In 1197, when Richard Coeur de Lion demanded that his ecclesiastical tenants-in-chief should provide him with knight service overseas, Hugh of Lincoln refused. He was dismissed from the King's Council and the temporalities of his diocese were confiscated. Hugh crossed to Normandy and tracked King Richard down to his new castle, Chateau Gaillard. He found him hearing Mass. At first the King refused to acknowledge Hugh, until he seized him by the tunic and shook him, demanding the customary kiss of greeting. After that relationships were somewhat restored. Hugh seems to have been held in awe as an ascetic and charismatic holy man whom no-one dared challenge.

Today the tangible result of Hugh's episcopate is to be seen in the Church he rebuilt after the earthquake of 1185. In charge of the building work, Hugh put a brilliant and inspired young English master-mason from Northamptonshire, Geoffrey de Noiers. He replaced the ruins of the Romanesque church of Remigius with a superb Gothic building. The pointed arches at Lincoln were among the first to be seen in England. The use of Purbeck Marble was also an innovation. The east end, or choir, rather than the nave, was always the first part of a church to be built, so that the divine liturgy could be maintained. The foundations of Hugh's new choir were laid in 1192. 53 years after his death in 1200 the great design was brought to completion. It was not until well into the thirteenth century that work began on the nave. Donations came in slowly, perhaps because lay people regarded the new east end as for the benefit of the clergy. Scholarly opinion is that the canons deliberately set out to emphasise the contrast between the new choir built according to the 'most advanced structural and aesthetic ideas of the time' and the old-fashioned and dilapidated Romanesque nave. It is possible that Hugh's personal Carthusian austerity was troubled by the extravagance of the new choir. Nevertheless, he founded St Mary's Guild, whose members undertook to contribute 1,000 marks a year to the fabric fund and he promised generous indulgences to all who would give. What is more, the Bishop is depicted as lending a hand himself in the building, heaving a hod with his own hands.

While this story may be true, it may also be part of the legend of Hugh deliberately fostered by the canons to stimulate lay support for the building work. The miraculous properties of Hugh's hod played a part in the process leading to his canonisation. Hugh died in the evening of 16 November 1200 in the house of the Bishops of Lincoln in the Temple in London, exhausted after an arduous pilgrimage back to La Grande Chartreuse, and the cares of office. Before he died he called his faithful architect Geoffrey to his bedside, requesting him to complete the Chapel of St John the Baptist, patron saint of the Carthusians. This was on the east side of the north choir transept, thus indicating how far work had progressed.

The embalmed body was brought to Lincoln after a four-day journey, during which the candles burned continuously around the bier 'so that they were never at any time without the light of one of the tapers although the weather was unusually bad on account of the wind and rain'. As the cortège approached Lincoln, the bells of the Cathedral and all the city's churches began to ring. The Jews of Lincoln came out to meet the Bishop who had loved them. In the mud and rain King John of England and King William of Scotland (long a friend of Hugh) and certain English earls carried Hugh's body into his Cathedral Church in the presence of the Archbishops of Canterbury, York, and Dubrovnik, thirteen bishops, and other ecclesiastics and nobility. Hugh's chaplain, Adam, arrayed the body in the vestments Hugh had worn at his consecration and he was laid to rest before the altar of St John the Baptist as he had requested.

There was a general feeling that a saint had just died. Other cathedrals had their saints. There had been plans for the canonisation of the first Norman bishop, Remy. Now Hugh would be the saint for Lincoln. So many came to the tomb that the Chapel of St John the Baptist had to be enlarged. Nevertheless, it was not until King John's reign was over that moves could begin to canonise Hugh. For part of that time the realm had been under Papal Interdict and no divine services could be said for six years. Rome did not issue the Bull authorising the canonisation until 1220. His feast was to be kept on 17 November, the liturgical anniversary of his death.

By this time the body of Thomas à Becket had been translated to a new shrine in Canterbury Cathedral. The canons of Lincoln were not to be outdone in building a shrine worthy of the earthly remains of a great saint, and likely to attract crowds of pilgrims. Notwithstanding the misappropriation of 11,000 marks from the building fund by the barons during their civil war against King John, the scaffolding of the nave was moving inexorably west. In 1235 Robert Grosseteste, the Chancellor of the University of Oxford, a great scholar, patron of the Franciscan friars and of the scientific investigations of Friar Roger Bacon, and once a poor deacon in Hugh of Lincoln's household, was presented to the see. Bishop Grosseteste was no mild liberal but a fierce disciplinarian, enforcing Catholic orthodoxy. He not only put up the backs of the canons, but also clashed with King and Pope, travelling to Rome at the age of 80 to defend his views. In spite of the collapse of the central tower in 1239, the nave, western (or nave) transepts, and western chapels were completed in his time (although the great arch of the western vestibule is not central to the west towers). During his episcopate a state entrance called the Galilee Porch was made for the Bishop on the west side of the south transept.

'For more than 60 years', wrote the former Subdean, Canon Cook, 'the cathedral planned by St Hugh had been building and had never been free from masons, marblers, carpenters and joiners in great numbers. In the precincts had been a constant coming and going of carts and wagons conveying marble, stone, timber and other materials to the site. The canons and priest-vicars had patiently endured the noise, bustle and smother inseparable from building operations and now the cathedral was finished perhaps they might anticipate an undisturbed quiet such as they had never enjoyed at Lincoln.'

It was not to be. The chapter now embarked on a project to pull down St Hugh's east end beyond the high altar and replace his florette of radiating chapels by a retro-choir with a squared east end in the English tradition. In 1255 the canons were given Royal permission to break through part of the city defences to make room for the proposed enlargement of the Cathedral. In this extension, immediately behind the high altar, on 6 October 1280, in the presence of King Edward I, his Queen, Eleanor of Castile, the King's brother, the Queen of Navarre, the Earls of Gloucester, Lincoln, and Warwick, the Archbishop of Canterbury, and many other nobles and bishops, the remains of St Hugh were translated from their original resting place in the Chapel of

St John the Baptist to the new and costly shrine embellished with precious stones. The conduits of the city ran with wine. Perhaps to profit from two shrines, the canons placed St Hugh's head separately, in a gold jewel-encrusted reliquary, and set it on a pedestal apart from the shrine where the body was. Day and night this was watched by keepers. The irony, probably, would not have been lost on Hugh, who was himself an inveterate collector of the relics of saints. In 1364 thieves got away with the head casket, jettisoning the head in a field and selling the precious reliquary in London. On their way home to Lincoln they in their turn were robbed and were later caught and hanged. A crow, it is said, kept guard over the head in the field until it was found and restored to the Cathedral, to be enclosed in a new reliquary.

There the saint's bones remained for almost two centuries, surrounded by thirty angels high in the Angel Choir, playing their music, in a sculptured heaven that can be entered by passing beneath the figure of Christ seated in majesty above the Judgement Porch, judging those who are able to pass through into the bliss within and those who must be cast into outer darkness.

There are many other notable people buried in the Cathedral. In the nave alone there are at least eighty-seven tombs. There are also thirty-six chantry chapels. The viscera of Queen Eleanor of Castile are buried here, as well as the bones of, among many others, Bishop Henry Burghersh, Chancellor of England, his brother Bartholomew, who fought with the Black Prince at Crècy, Katherine Swynford, third wife of John of Gaunt, whose son Henry Beaufort was Bishop of Lincoln and later a Cardinal, and from whom the Tudor monarchs descended. Besides the shrine of St Hugh, there were four shrines of other saints and tombs of bishops noted for their saintliness, especially Bishop John de Dalderby, whose episcopate (1300–1320) saw the Angel Choir completed. He also granted indulgences to all who contributed towards the completion of the final stages of the central tower. Work began in 1307 and by 1311 the tallest central tower in England was ready for the bells. Until 1548 it was surmounted by a wooden spire. Even without its spire, the Cathedral is visible from miles away:

'Great monument of Love Divine
Thou Lincoln on thy sovereign hill.'

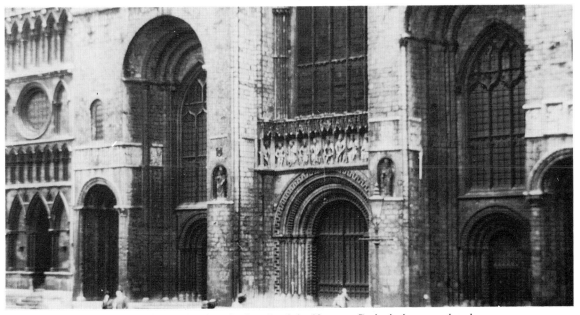

The west front, showing the facade of the Norman Cathedral encapsulated
in its Gothic frame.

39

ABOVE: The east end, which replaced Hugh of Lincoln's chevette of chapels, to accommodate his two shrines. BELOW: The Exchequer Gate held the Dean and Chapter's financial records, including the registers of their many estates. LEFT: The story of the Swineherd of Stow who gave his wages to St Hugh's building fund was part of a fund-raising campaign to encourage ordinary people to make gifts to the fabric.

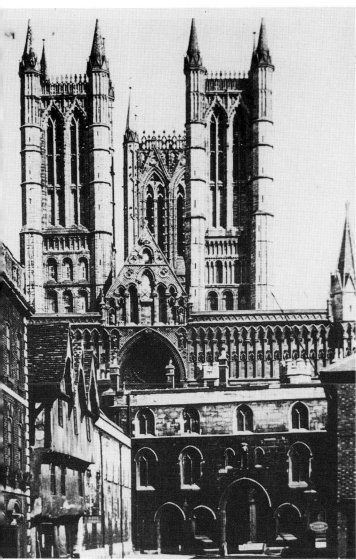

LEFT: When curfew was rung the Exchequer Gate was one of those which shut off Minster Yard. RIGHT: The Chapel of St Mary Magdalen, once the parish church, also called the Morning Chapel, may have served as Chapter House. BELOW: St Hugh's Choir.

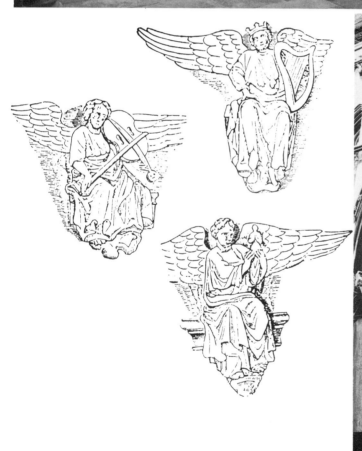

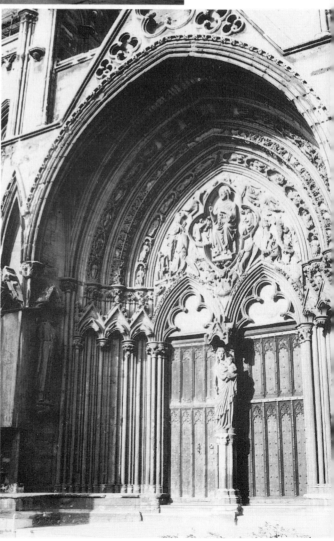

OPPOSITE ABOVE: The Cloister from the north. The steep hillside did not allow one on the conventional sunny south. LEFT: The heavenly host praising God and saying 'Holy, Holy, Holy . . .', high in the Angel Choir. RIGHT: The Judgement Porch. ABOVE LEFT: The exterior of the chantry chapel for masses to be sung for Bishop Longland, unfinished because of the Reformation. Its eastern wall pierces the stomach of the female figure. RIGHT: Vicars Court, looking north towards the gatehouse. BELOW: The great barn for the Dean and Chapter's tithes.

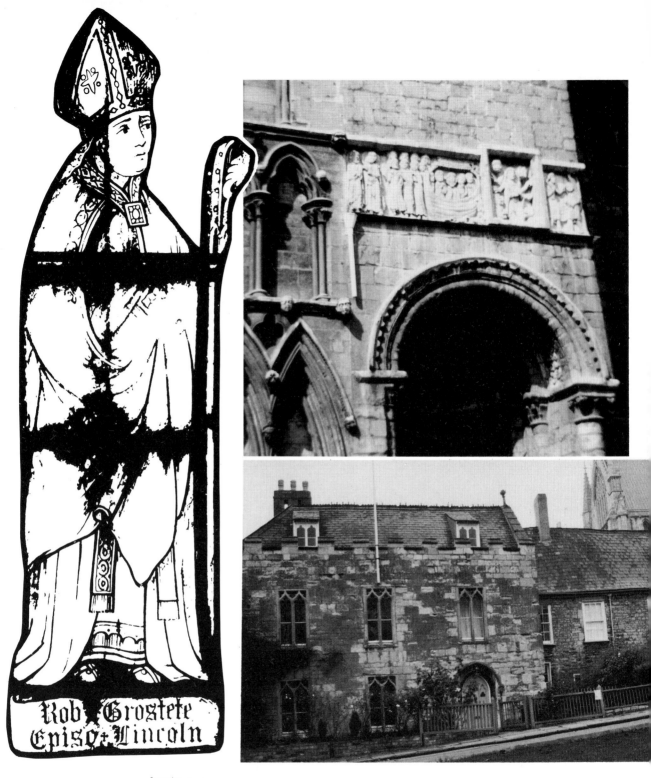

LEFT: Robert Grosseteste, Bishop 1235–53; a nearly contemporary portrait in the east window of the Lady Chapel of the parish church of Lea-by-Gainsborough. RIGHT: Fragments of the frieze tell the Salvation History in pictures. It formerly ran round the entire exterior of the Norman Cathedral. BELOW: The house of the priests of Lord Cantelupe's Chantry, founded in 1355.

44

ABOVE: The Chapter House, where the Dean and canons meet in Chapter to administer the life of the foundation. LEFT: Pottergate Arch, one of the gates into the Close, dating from 1328. RIGHT: Tower on the Close Wall in Winnowsty, c1319, one of four surviving.

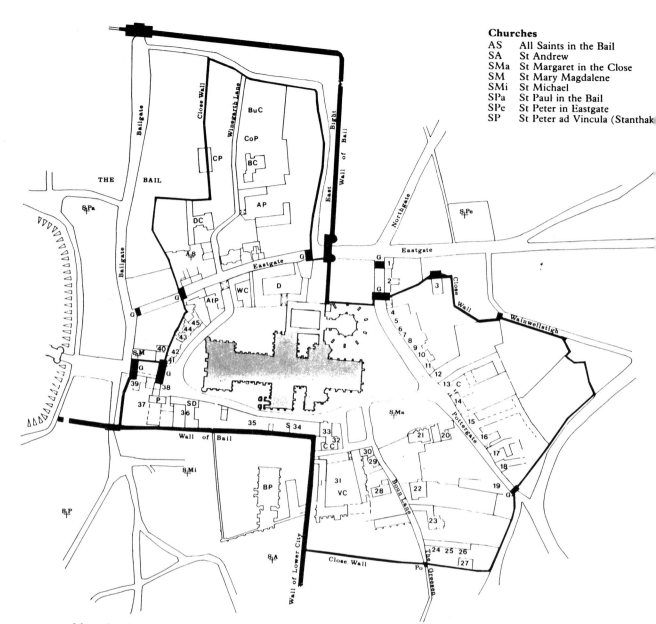

Churches
AS All Saints in the Bail
SA St Andrew
SMa St Margaret in the Close
SM St Mary Magdalene
SMi St Michael
SPa St Paul in the Bail
SPe St Peter in Eastgate
SP St Peter ad Vincula (Stanthak

Map showing the relationship between Close and City Walls. **Houses without survey numbers —** AP Atherstone Place; AtP Atton Place; BC Burghersh Chantry; BP Bishop's Palace; BuC Burton Chantry (Burton Place); CoP Coleby Place; CP Cottesford Place; D Deanery, now Cathedral School; DC Deloraine Court; WC Works Chantry. Gates in the wall of the Close indicated by G. The postern gate in the Greesen marked by Po. **Survey numbers —** *Fascicule I:* 1 4 Priorygate, including the Rest; 2 3 Priorygate, the former Elephant Inn; 3 2 Minster Yard, the Priory; 4 3 Minster Yard; 5 4 Minster Yard; 6 5 Minster Yard; 7 5a Minster Yard; 8 6 Minster Yard; 9 7 Minster Yard; 10 8 Minster Yard; 11 9 Minster Yard; 12 10 Minster Yard, former Choristers' House; 13 11 Minster Yard (C), the Chancery; 14 12 Minster Yard, part of Graveley Place; 15 5 Pottergate; 16 4 Pottergate; 17 3 Pottergate; 18 2 Pottergate. *Fascicule II:* 19 Site of former 1 Pottergate; 20 13 Minster Yard; 21 14 Minster Yard; 22 3 Greestone Place; 23 4 Greestone Place, Greestone House; 24 1 Greestone Terrace; 25 2 Greestone Terrace; 26 3 Greestone Terrace; 27 Greestone Mount; 28 2 Greestone Place; 29 1 Greestone Place; 30 15 Minster Yard; 31 Vicars' Court (VC); 32/33 Cantilupe Chantry (CC); 34 Site of house of the Sacrist; 35 Site of house/stables; 36 17 Minster Yard (SD), now Deanery; 37/38 18 Minster Yard (P), now in part Subdeanery; 39 2 Exchequergate; 40 Exchequergate Lodge; 41 19 Minster Yard; 42 20 Minster Yard; 43 21 Minster Yard; 44 22 Minster Yard; 45 23 Minster Yard.

Greens and Scarlets

Today, on a Royal visit to Lincoln, the Mayor will welcome the Sovereign into the city and surrender the symbol of authority, the sword, as a sign that the Mayor keeps the city for the Crown. The Sovereign then ceremonially hands it back, thereby indicating that the authority vested in the Mayor may be retained during the Crown's presence in the city. When the Mayor goes to the Cathedral on Christmas Eve to give the Christmas message, the Dean welcomes him or her, the congregation stands to receive its chief citizen, and the Mayor in robes and chain, preceded by the city Sheriff and then by the sword-bearer, wearing the cap of maintenance, and the sergeant-at-mace, must be the last to enter and take her or his appointed place, before the Dean and Chapter and Bishop's processions enter (preceded in their case by the great Chapter Cross). The Mayor is often referred to as the 'chief citizen', a title that connotes more than simply a city-dweller. The office of Mayor represents the liberties and privileges won to manage their own affairs by the citizens of Lincoln and the powers vested in them by the Crown over the centuries. In the twelfth century, however, there was no such office.

The upheavals of Stephen's reign were followed by a century of strong government and prosperity under the Angevin kings. This was parallelled by a growth of urban life. In some places new towns were created; elsewhere old-established market centres were developed and granted valuable rights giving them control over their own affairs. The powers extended to these new urban communities were recorded in documents called charters, issued either by the King or the lord of the manor.

For an ancient city like Lincoln, these rights originated not in a charter but, as the saying was, before the memory of man. Moreover, while the new generation of towns were freeing themselves from their feudal lords, Lincoln still came under the authority of the Royal Bailiff. In 1194, therefore, the citizens bought a charter from Richard I for 500 marks (about the sum due to the King from three freemen) obtaining the same customs as held by Northampton or London. It was usual for the customs of other towns to serve as models in this way and this shows that Lincoln wanted the best. This first charter allowed the freemen to hold the burwarmot once a week, so defending in writing what had hitherto been an unwritten custom. Freemen of Lincoln were exempted from the need to plead before any court outside the city, except in the case of land ownership. Moreover, they were empowered to elect a bailiff of their own choosing to work with the King's Bailiff. They were exempted from the 'murdrum' (the collective responsibility for the murder of a Frenchman) and were free to trade in any market town in the Kingdom without paying toll and lastage. If anyone demanded these dues from the men of Lincoln without making restitution, the Bailiff could distrain upon the goods of merchants coming there from the offending town.

As well as the written confirmation of ancient rights, the citizens had gained important new freedoms which significantly enlarged the definition of a freeman. A freeman was now only answerable to the court of his own city, *ie*: to his fellow freemen; he could elect one of his number to act to protect the rights of the freemen alongside the Royal Bailiff. Of course the charter makes no reference to the electoral procedure at this early period. Six years later the citizens secured another charter from Richard's brother, John, at a cost of 300 marks, confirming their existing freedoms and adding the right to elect four coroners (who, as their title implies, were to protect the rights of the Crown) and *two* Bailiffs (or Provosts, a title suggesting a policing role). The right to choose these officers, including even the representatives of the King, from their own ranks, marks an important stage in the development of the city's freedom from outside interference. Fifteen years later, charters like this provided a model for Magna Carta and supplied the language of representation and consent which American colonists were to invoke. What was happening in Lincoln in 1200 reflects what was happening at another level. The feudal system, if it ever existed outside the pages of treatises, was giving way to a relationship based, not on divine right of King over subject, but on the rights of subjects under the King.

This is what the office of Mayor, the chief citizen of Lincoln, stands for. It is an office held under the Crown, whence it derives its authority, symbolised by mace and sword, to hold the city for the Crown, and yet the Mayor, as chief citizen, embodies the rights of self-determination, represented by the mace, obtained for the town from the Crown by the freemen. The office of Mayor derives from early town government in France. It is first heard of by that name in Lincoln in 1206, when the Mayor took the place of the alderman as head of the Gild.

From the beginning the Mayors were attended by their bedells, a medieval English word, (in French, sergeants) meaning a herald, officer, or attendant who carried a mace, waited on the Mayor, served writs and other legal documents, and arrested wrongdoers. When Richard II visited Lincoln in 1386 he granted the Mayor the right to have a sword of state borne before him and almost certainly presented the city with the fourteenth century fighting sword, bearing Edward III's coat of arms, which is still the city state sword. The city sword bearer is sometimes called 'the king's (or queen's)sword-bearer'. There are two other city state swords, one the gift of Henry VII when he visited Lincoln after his defeat of Lambert Simnel's rebellion at Stoke by Newark in 1487, the other, some believe is the gift of Charles I when he came to Lincoln at the outbreak of the Civil War.

The sergeants had begun to carry a mace by 1422 and the mace-bearer was sometimes referred to as 'the common sergeant-at-mace of the lord king'. The Corporation's large mace, of silver gilt, belongs to the time of the Restoration in 1660. A small silver mace belonging to the time of Cromwell is by custom carried before the city Sheriff. However, people are most familiar with the Mayor's chain of office. The oldest, no longer worn, was bought in 1849 for the visit of Prince Albert to the city, on his way to open Grimsby Dock. It was replaced in 1960 by the chain now in use. The oldest chain, of 1710, is that worn by the Deputy Mayor (who becomes Mayor in the following year).

On ceremonial occasions the sword-bearer wears the velvet cap of maintenance, first mentioned in 1534, and a jealously guarded privilege since, after the Wars of the Roses, livery and maintenance were expressly banned to reduce the power of overmighty subjects. Only persons of a certain rank and wealth were supposed to wear velvet hats. Sometimes, however, the Mayor himself carried the sword and wore the cap of maintenance, for instance when William III visited Lincoln in 1695. A few years before the cap of maintenance is first heard of, the Mayor of Nottingham addressed the Mayor of Lincoln as 'Right Worshipful' and this title is still used.

About the time that the office of Mayor of Lincoln is first recorded, the common purse, that is financial means provided by the citizens themselves or derived from sources to which they were collectively entitled, makes its first appearance. At the same time Lincoln acquired a common seal, to be affixed to the documents expressing the common or corporate acts of the city. In those days Mayor-making on the Feast of Holy Cross, 14 September, marked the beginning of the civic year, culminating with the Feast of St Anne and the great Corpus Christi procession and pageants at the end of July. Between these two events it was the Mayor's duty to promote the annual cycle of civic ceremonial. His powers might also be extra-municipal as when, in 1521, he solemnly pronounced a curse on whoever had improperly removed the city records.

Lincoln was a wealthy city and everyone knows that Robin Hood and his merry men camouflaged themselves in Lincoln Green. Lincoln's prosperity rested largely on its place in the highly profitable trade in wool and woollen cloth for which England was famous. However, the city was principally known, not for Lincoln Green, but for a cloth called Lincoln Scarlet. Scarlet was not its colour but referred to its quality as a finely finished cloth. In the reign of Henry II as many as 200 spinners were employed in the city. The wool came in from the flocks owned by abbeys like Barlings, which maintained a warehouse in Lincoln. The woollen cloth of Lincoln was worn not only by the legendary outlaws of Sherwood Forest but was purchased for the dress and household furnishings of the King and his great barons (including, it may be, the Sheriff of Nottingham), making the city's woolmen among the most rich and important merchants, not only in England but in northern Europe.

Such was William Cause, Bailiff of Lincoln in 1263 and 1279, Mayor in 1298, and chosen to represent the city in the Parliament of 1295. He traded at the great fair of St Ives in Huntingdonshire. In 1273 he had a special licence to export wool during the war with Flanders. Grander still was Stephen of Stanham, a Lincoln draper or cloth dealer. Twice Mayor during the early fourteenth century, he traded in Lincoln and also had a shop or stall in London. Stephen was an official merchant to the king, acting as purveyor of wax (for the Royal seal and candles), sugar, spice 'and all things nice', as well as the cloth which was his speciality, to the Royal wardrobe. When Parliament met in Lincoln in 1301 he supplied the Royal household, providing sugar, figs and fish for the seventeen-year-old Prince Edward. He attended the great fairs of St Ives and Boston, and owned a ship which sailed out of Boston to Flanders. The links which modern Lincoln has with Bruges were already foreshadowed by these Lincoln merchants.

Altogether twenty Lincoln merchants were to be found attending the St Ives Fairs from 1270–1324, of whom six held civic office. In 1278 William of Wickenby travelled by boat from Lincoln to St Ives to trade in horse carcasses. So strongly represented were Lincoln merchants that they maintained a permanent presence at St Ives and Winchester, renting 30 shops on the fairgrounds. Not that their presence was always peaceful. In 1241 Lincoln men were implicated with other English merchants in a fight with traders from Ypres. In 1327 Edward III gave the city the right to hold its own annual fair, although this does not seem to have achieved the prominence of Boston or St Ives.

We must beware of allowing the wool business to efface other trades and crafts. St Cuthbert's in the Bullring was referred to as 'ad Forum bladi', (by the cornmarket), and a poultry market was held nearby. A weekly market and annual fair were held in Newport; the market cross stood in the street before the Church of St John. It was prudent at the commencement of each reign for the city to obtain confirmation from the new King of it's liberties and privileges. Thus at his first Parliament, held at Lincoln in 1327, Edward III confirmed the city's existing Monday, Wednesday and Friday markets. Stalls were also set up in the Castle ditch and the Cathedral close although, since these were outside the jurisdiction of the city authorities, they were a source of dispute. In 1316 Edward II had granted the citizens the right to weigh and measure all wares sold on the city market and the profits arising from the assize of bread and ale by which freemen were chosen to inspect the public brewhouses and bakehouses. Any baker who adulterated his or her bread or pies with chalk or bran, or any brewer who watered the ale would be punished. Brewers and bakers could only pursue their trades if they were licensed by the Mayor and Bailiffs.

Surnames derived from urban occupations in the Subsidy Roll of 1332 account for nearly a tenth of all names and indicate at least fifty different occupations. Among these were the potteries on the outskirts, turning out a sandy ware, mainly for local use. A kiln near the east gate was producing Lincoln shelly ware as early as the tenth century. By the end of the fourteenth century (when the city's commercial life was no longer at its height) there were eleven guilds, representing barbers, masons, tilers, cordwainers, fullers, weavers, mercers, archers, sailors, minstrels and actors. There is also a danger, because the records become more plentiful, of seeing Lincoln's commercial greatness as entirely a product of the twelfth and thirteenth centuries, whereas the history of Lincoln's gild merchant probably began before the Norman Conquest.

Henry II laid down that all merchants seeking to trade in Lincolnshire, no matter what their trade, had to belong to the gild merchant of Lincoln. Originally the alderman presided over this institution, which was dominated by a small group of wealthy Lincoln businessmen, from whose ranks the Bailiffs usually came. In due course burwarmot meetings were moved indoors from the mootstone to the hall of the gild merchant, implying that by then the gildsmen controlled it. The city council originated as a caucus of merchant members of the burwarmot. There was frequent friction between the weavers, fullers and dyers and the other trades who controlled the gild merchant. In 1290 and again in 1293 the high-handed actions of the mafia of powerful merchants who ran the city led to open conflict. On the latter occasion the strife between 'the high and mighty persons of the city and the king's middling subjects thereof' over the control of executive power led to street disturbances and the intervention of the King. Until the fourteenth century the leading families in Lincoln were a property-owning rentier group, indistinguishable from the rural gentry. Between a third and a half of the wealthier inhabitants were immigrants from within a radius of 30 miles. Aliens included John the Fleming, Ralf of Rouen, Simon of Arras, and Eustace le Hauser.

Lincoln's prosperity depended upon communications. The old Roman roads were still in use in the eleventh century, although the Great North Road replaced the Ermine Street as the main north-south route, by-passing Lincoln in the fourteenth century. The Fosse Way from Lincoln to Newark provided the feeder road to the Great North Road. Bishop Hugh's journey to Lincoln took eight days. After Queen Eleanor died the King's journey to London also lasted eight days. These were the great ones, with large retinues, able to protect themselves from the bands of thieves who infested the highway between Newark and Lincoln. Other travellers, caught on the road at nightfall, could take refuge at the halfway house on Swinderby Moor, provided by the Prior of the Knights Hospitallers at Eagle. Much traffic went by water, either by the Witham to the sea at Boston or along the Fossdyke to the Trent at Torksey, which functioned as an outport of Lincoln. Torksey ranked next to Lincoln as a borough in the Domesday Survey, having had 213 burgesses on the eve of the Conquest although, perhaps as a result of the Conqueror's harrying of the north in 1069–70, there were only 106 by 1086 and many properties were standing waste.

In 1326 Lincoln was designated one of fourteen Staple towns where all wool, hides, skins, tin, and timber had to pass through the customs before they could be exported. English and foreign merchants trading through the Staple formed a fellowship which chose a Mayor who acted for the King in collecting duties. The Staple was located inside the wall of the city, near the Thornbridge on the Witham. The Mayor of the Staple presided over the Court of the Staple that dealt with trade disputes. The wool that passed through the Lincoln staple had to be weighed on the 'steelyard', or weigh beam, by the *ponderator*, assisted by four freemen of the city responsible for tolls and customs.

However, this prosperity did not last. In 1332 there were only 433 taxpayers and by 1334 the city had slipped to seventh place in the Kingdom, supplanted by Boston; the Staple was taken away from Lincoln in 1369. In 1348, the year before the Black Death reached Lincoln, the city's weavers were forced to seek relief from their annual payment to the Exchequer. They had been getting deeper in arrears since 1321. By then says, the cloth which formed Lincoln's biggest output, was no longer sold at the fairs and Lincoln's merchants had ceased to maintain their shops at Winchester and St Ives. Part of the cause of Lincoln's difficulties may have been the slowing down in the economy, which began in the later decades of the previous century. However, perhaps most important was the shift of cloth manufacture away from Lincoln to new water-powered fulling mills located on fast-flowing upland rivers.

The Black Death was rife in Lincolnshire in 1349. In Lincoln, where sixty per cent of the clergy died in the epidemic, of 295 wills disposing of burgage tenements in the city between 1315 and 1376, about a third were enrolled in the Burwarmot Book in the plague year 1349 alone, equivalent to thirty normal years. By 1360 the city's decayed condition, the evil name of its merchants, its filthy state, and the dilapidated condition of its walls and towers drew comment from Edward III. By 1390 the gildhall had been pulled down. The new one stood unfinished until the King compelled the city to complete it in 1500, perhaps to ensure that the government of his city was not carried on in private houses. Nevertheless, 'to save the city from destruction', in 1409 Lincoln was created a county in its own right, allowed to elect two Sheriffs in place of the Bailiffs, and the Mayor became the Royal Escheator, authorised to take into his custody the King's property in the city in the event of the demise of a Crown tenant or the forfeiture of an estate to the King. A new fair was granted, to last for two weeks on either side of the feast of St Hugh (17 November).

This did little to alleviate Lincoln's difficulties and tax relief had to be allowed for several years. In 1447 letters patent were issued permitting the authorities to acquire property, and granting remission of taxation for forty years. The property purchased was the manor of Canwick, worth 40 shillings a year. In 1463 Branston, Waddington, Bracebridge, and Canwick were taken out of Lincolnshire to be incorporated into the county of the city of Lincoln. In 1484 Washingborough, Heighington, Fiskerton, Greetwell, Burton and Cherry Willingham were similarly added by Richard III but, with the accession of the House of Tudor, all his acts were annulled. When a Subsidy was taken in 1524, Lincoln, once third city in the kingdom, could only yield £298 to the King, making it nineteenth among English towns.

Chestnuts in Bishop Grosseteste College grounds — said by some to mark the ancient boundary of the city. Beyond them is the line of the 'King's Ditch'.

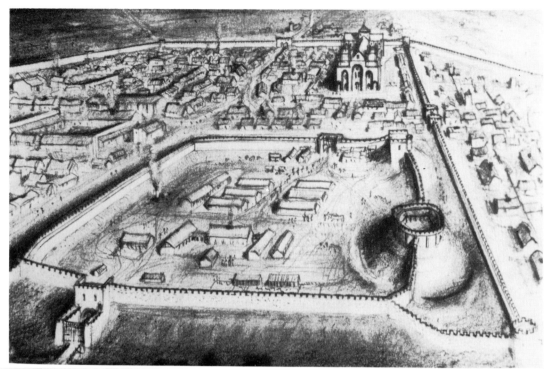

ABOVE: Impression of the twelfth century upper city, including the
new northern suburb of Newport. BELOW: The Great Bargate — the
southernmost entry into the city.

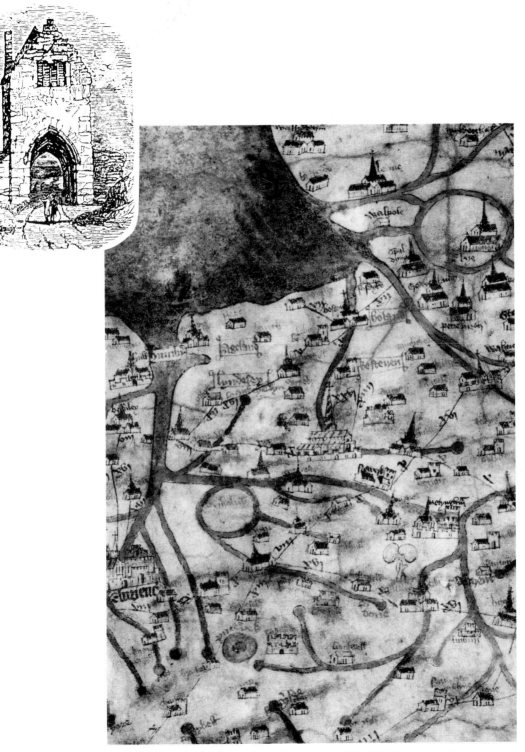

LEFT: The Newland Gate, now disappeared. BELOW: Lincoln, as depicted
on the Gough Map, showing the medieval road links.

53

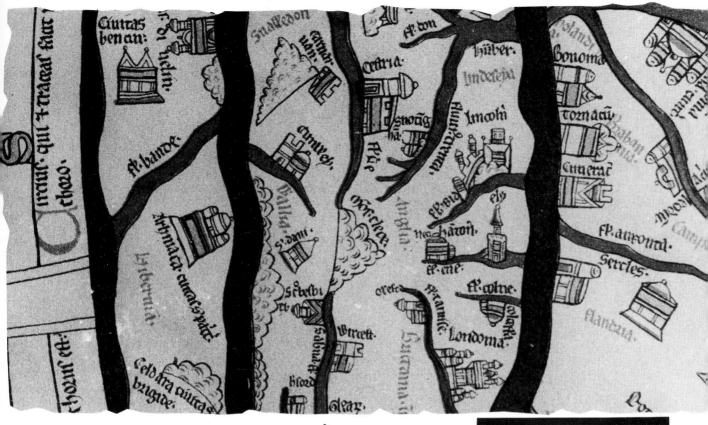

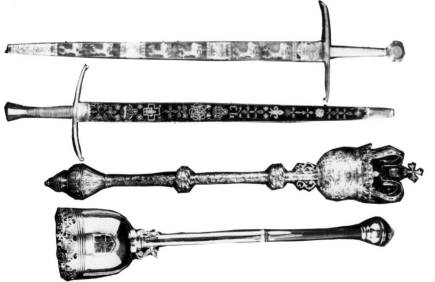

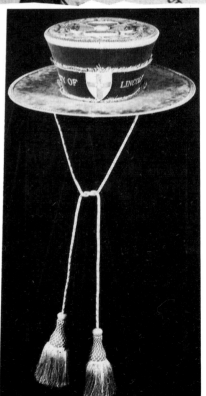

ABOVE: Lincoln, in the Hereford *Mappa Mundi*, drawn by a canon who originated from Lincolnshire. The central spire of the cathedral on its hill is clearly shown. BELOW: The fourteenth century Richard II Sword of state which is borne before the Mayor; the Henry VII 'Lent' Sword, carried before the Mayor in Lent; the Mace, of silver gilt, from the Restoration and the oldest surviving Mace, the City Sheriff's, dating from Cromwell's time. RIGHT: The Cap of Maintenance, known to have been worn by the sword-bearer since at least 1534.

LEFT: The City Waits' Chain of 1710, now worn by the Deputy Mayor.
RIGHT: The City Common Seal of 1449, rediscovered in the British
Museum in 1900. BELOW: The Stonebow, or gate, housing the Guildhall,
seat of the City Council since 1500.

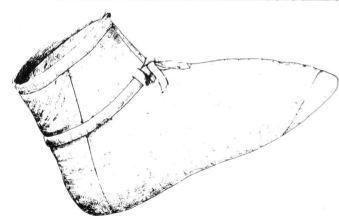

ABOVE LEFT: The Mayor's Chair, limit of the city's jurisdiction below the Close and Castle. RIGHT: The Mayor, Cllr David Chambers, tenders the Richard II Sword to HM Queen Elizabeth II in 1980. BELOW LEFT: Late eleventh century leather boot, from Waterside North. RIGHT: The Jewish community lived in houses like this.

LEFT: Erroneously called Aaron's House, this building recalls one of the principal financiers of twelfth century England. RIGHT: A medieval caricature of Aaron of Lincoln anticipates Nazi propaganda. BELOW: Bellaset of Wallingford, executed for forgery in 1290, lived here, in the Jews House.

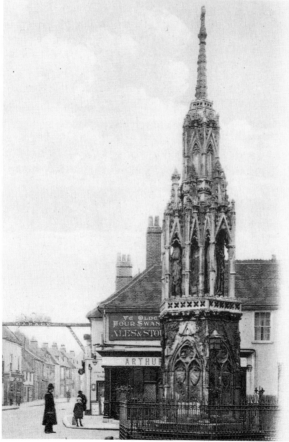

ABOVE LEFT: Jew's Court has been identified as the synagogue of medieval Lincoln. RIGHT: The shrine of Little St Hugh was a focus for medieval anti-semitism. A child's skeleton was found when the tomb was opened in 1791. BELOW LEFT: Queen Eleanor died of a fever at Harby in Nottinghamshire. Where the cortège halted on its journey south the King ordered Eleanor Crosses set up. The first, at Cross o' Cliff in Lincoln, was destroyed in 1648. This one is at Waltham in Essex. RIGHT: Statues of Edward I and Queen Eleanor on the south side of the Angel Choir. He summoned Parliament to Lincoln in 1301.

All God's Houses

In the early eighteenth century Daniel Defoe visited Lincoln and found thirteen churches, 'but the meanest to look on that are anywhere to be seen'. He was told that once there had been as many as fifty-two. This was probably an exaggeration since, evidence has only been found for forty-six by the beginning of the thirteenth century.

The law of pre-Conquest England declared that, if a landowner aspired to the rank of thegn, he had to own a church on his estate. Several of the oldest churches in Lincoln seem to have originated in this way, as private chapels founded by property-owners. A verdict given in Nottingham in 1086 said that no licence was needed to build a church. Thus All Saints-in-the-Bail (now defunct) belonged to Godric, son of Garewic, whose estate consisted of twelve tofts, or house plots, and four crofts or gardens. St Peter-at-Pleas in the High Street (also defunct) was possibly founded by Earl Leofric of Mercia, descending to Earl Morcar and then, after the Conquest, to Earl Roger of Poitou, who gave this together with his other churches in Lincolnshire to St Martin's Abbey, Sees in Normandy. Likewise Tochi, son of Outi, had a part-share in St Peter-at-Arches. It served his hall and household and the occupants of his thirty tenancies. Tochi also owned two other city churches.

Another landowner who built churches on his city property was Colsuen, who founded St Peter-at-the-Spring (or Wells — now defunct) in Bagholme on the east of the city, perhaps as part of the development of this suburb. He may also have built another church to the south, dedicated to St Augustine (defunct). St Mary-le-Wigford bears a much worn inscription testifying that Eirtag built the church. St Michael-on-the-Mount belonged to Agemund the priest, who held the rank of thegn.

Although only five churches are mentioned in the Domesday Book, Lincoln was one of the most important towns in the Kingdom and altogether perhaps thirty-five churches existed in Lincoln then, built by thegns of the shire or well-to-do burgesses, in the shadow cast by the expectation of the millenium and the end of the world. It was indeed true, as William of Malmesbury wrote, that a man counted the time lost that he did not make some benefaction, and churches rose everywhere. Nevertheless, churches were regarded by their founders as valuable assets, much as the woodland and mills on their estates. Under pre-Conquest law they were endowed with land called 'the glebe' and an income in kind from the parishioners called 'tithe' (a tenth). The living of the vicarage of St Mary-le-Wigford in Lincoln, including tithes from all the inhabitants amounted, in the seventeenth century, to £8 10s 0d (£8.50 in modern terms). The vicar also received the tithe of the willow trees that grew on Sincil Bank. St Paul-in-the-Bail owned a malt mill and an eighth of an acre north of the churchyard called the Mintyard, which by 1679 had become a garden. Many of these churches were small. Some may even have been converted from secular buildings and doubled as warehouses between one Sunday and the next, especially in the case of St Mary-le-Wigford and St Peter-at-Gowts. Often they served only small clusters of houses.

By the twelfth century opinion was turning against lay control of God's property. In Lincoln this meant the Bishop acquired the right to take over all churches in the city whose priests held their title from the King. Bishops used this power to lay claim to any church where the ownership was in doubt. A century later a jury found that, although many churches had formerly been owned by citizens, they had failed to answer the King's summons to defend their possession and so they had passed into the King's hands and thence to the Bishop.

The churches mentioned in 1086 were St Lawrence, St Mary, All Saints, St Michaels, and St Peter. This was probably the church of St Peter-at-Pleas which stood by the mootstone in the High Street, on what was called Mikelgate. A church that existed then, although not mentioned in the Domesday Survey, was St Mark in the suburb of Wigford, founded in the tenth century and, to judge from its graveyard, a church serving a parish from the start. Its foundation is further evidence of the growth of Lincoln then, while the later enlargement of the churchyard and reconstruction of the church point to population increases in the late tenth century. After destruction by fire in 1120 St Mark's was rebuilt in as grand a manner as any in the city, a mark of the wealth in this part of Lincoln. Another pre-Conquest church not referred to in the Domesday Survey was St Peter-at-Arches, in Briggate which, in the twelfth century, became the property of the Austin canons of Shelford in Nottinghamshire. St Benedict's, known as St Bene't of Wigford, was presented to the Cathedral before 1107. The architecture of St Mary-le-Wigford, with a tower in the typical Lincolnshire Anglo-Saxon tradition, indicates that this church too was standing at the time of the Domesday Survey. Although St Peter-at-Gowts, further down the Ermine Street, is not recorded until 1147, its tower shows that it also existed at the time of the Norman Conquest. St Martin was the patron saint of Lincoln in the tenth century and it is likely that a church in the High Street dedicated to him was another early church as was St Margaret-in-Pottergate, on land south-east of the Cathedral, and which stood in the way of the extension of the building of St Hugh's shrine. A lead plate, found in 1847, recorded the burial of Siford the priest of St Helen and St Margaret (the only reference to a church dedicated to St Helen in Lincoln). Perhaps Siford was Siward the priest, one of the city lawmen of 1066. The west end of St Peter 'Stanthaket' (stone thatched, ie: stone roofed), *alias* St Peter-in-the-Skin Market, in Hungate, its land extending from the King's Highway to the barn of Leo the Jew, at the junction of Michaelgate and Springhill, has recently been dated to the mid-eleventh century.

Churches of the early twelfth century were All Saints-in-Hungate, which Henry I committed to Bishop Robert Bloet in 1114, St John-in-Newport which Bishop Alexander gave to one of the canons as his prebend in 1121, St Martin-in-the-Dernstall, recorded in 1190, and on Hungate, St Mary 'Crakepool'. A 'crake' was a waterfowl and so this was probably a reference to a pool on Newland near the Brayford. Also on low-lying land north of the Witham between the river and Saltergate lay St Swithun's parish, while south along the waterside was St Edmund's. We hear also of the parish of St Bartholomew, lying behind the Castle (in what are now the grounds of The Lawn) which the Abbey of Selby gave, with its glebe, to the Cathedral for the burial of the canons, because the Cathedral burial ground was so near the public street that the feet of passers-by trampled it, causing a health-hazard from the corruption so released. The Church itself had been ruined for some time and, as there were no parishioners, it was decided that its income should augment the maintenance of choir boys. Other churches were St George, St Cuthbert, Holy Trinity-below-Hill, St Faith-in-Newland, St Stephen-in-Midhergate (or Newland), Holy Trinity and St John, Holy Trinity and St Margaret, all in Wigford.

Often the dedications are some help in reconstructing the history of a church. Thus St Nicholas became popular after 1079 when his cult was established and this is a clue to the origin of St Nicholas-in-Newport, the suburb created after the Castle was built in 1068. St Clement, another suburban church, was a favourite Danish dedication, as was St Swithun, recalling the rich Danish commercial community. Another national dedication was to St Rumbold, a Flemish saint, a church built by the Flemish colony in the city. No street was without its church, which the people supported as they might a local team today. Even in 1526, when the city and its churches had reached a low ebb in their fortunes, there were over one hundred priests in Lincoln, not counting monks, nuns, friars, and men in minor orders.

From the thirteenth century the shrine of St Hugh of Lincoln became one of the most important pilgrim centres in northern Europe. On the feast of his canonisation crowds flocked to stand in awe and prayer before the tomb of one who, it was believed, stood before the throne of God interceding on their behalf. The sense of being at the Gate of Heaven was increased by the presence of the heavenly host in stone above them in the choir, and by the gorgeous colours and gold, silver and jewels which shone from the saint's earthly resting place. In 1267 the Papal Legate Ottobon preached a crusade in Lincoln and a great procession of clergy and people wound up the hill to the cathedral to hear his exhortation.

The wide open atrium in front of the cathedral formed a stage for the annual cycle of mystery plays, performed by the 'mysteries' or craft and trade guilds. This has been likened to putting on an Oberammergau every year. When, in 1311, the Church instituted the Feast of Corpus Christi throughout Christendom, it became necessary to find ways of explaining the theological meaning of the new feast to the largely uninstructed laity. Apart from the obligation to carry the Blessed Sacrament in procession from the mother church to the other parish churches, bishops were permitted to determine what form the celebration should take. In many places the guilds walked in the Corpus Christi processions, wearing their ceremonial liveries and carrying banners or other emblems of their crafts, and performing pageants just as they did on civic and other solemn occasions. In Lincoln a new guild was created, the guild of St Anne, patron saint of the Cathedral, to organise the festival. Everyone was nominally a member of St Anne's Guild. The cathedral clergy seem to have been responsible for performing the Coronation or Assumption of the Blessed Virgin Mary to end the Cycle. Otherwise, St Anne's Guild shared the organisation of the plays with the Corporation.

The Cathedral already had its East Sepulchre at which, no doubt, the East Morning dialogue between the three Maries and the angel at the tomb (*Matt 28, vv 1–7; Mark 16, vv 1–7*) took place, beginning 'Quem quaeritis in sepulchro, o Christicolae?' ('What seek ye at the tomb, oh little Christians?'). This would have been preceded by the enactment of the burial of Christ (the Deposition) on Good Friday and followed by the 'Peregrini' play on Easter Monday (when the Gospel reading concerns the walk to Emaus). The Lincoln Customs, or Use, were taken from Rouen, where such plays were certainly performed. In St Hugh's lifetime a reference occurs to an Easter play at the Abbey of Eynsham in Oxfordshire, of which he was patron, which derived from Lincoln. On the other hand, Bishop Grosseteste was no friend to the drama and ordered his archdeacons to suppress all miracle plays. Nevertheless the Galilee Porch of the Cathedral may have been so-called because part of the Easter drama took place there. In 1397 a Pater Noster or Morality play was mentioned at Lincoln. Nine years later the Cathedral clergy paid for costume materials for a play of the Prophets and the Annunciation and in 1420 the city allocated 8s 8d out of the tithes to buy things for a play. A private house was used for rehearsals in 1479. In 1521 every alderman was to make a gown for the kings in the pageant on St Anne's Day, and the Pater Noster play to be performed that year. Fifteen years later the Protestant Reformation killed all this. In 1537 the Bishop of Lincoln banned most annual feasts and holy days throughout his diocese, including patronal festivals (church holidays) and harvest holidays. Henceforth, with few holidays and no Feast of Corpus Christi, there would be no free time and no incentive to put on the Mystery Plays.

Before the Reformation, the Church's influence extended into all areas of the city's life and work. The sanatorium or hospital of the Holy Innocents for lepers, known as the Malandry, outside the city on land extending onto the South Common, was probably founded in the early twelfth century. The hospice of St Giles provided lodgings for elderly clergy. Outside the city walls to the south stood St Catherine's Priory, a double house for canons and canonesses of the order founded by St Gilbert of Sempringham in Lincolnshire, the only monastic order founded in medieval England.

Wherever there was a town there were the friars. Indeed, it has been said that without towns there would have been no friars. Lincoln was no exception. By 1300 the various orders of friars had houses there. The Greyfriars or Franciscans are traditionally held to have been brought to the city in about 1230 by Bishop Robert Grosseteste, who had come to admire them during his time as a teacher at Oxford. In 1301 there were 63 Franciscans attached to their house in the old gildhall (part of which now houses the City and County Museum). Their church probably stood on the north side of the convent precinct, which incorporated the whole south-east segment of the city. The Blackfriars, or Order of Preachers, founded by St Dominic, established a house of studies in Lincoln about the same time as the Franciscans. Theirs was the largest friary. Built in 1311, its location is thought to have been near to the present Sessions House. The Carmelites, or Whitefriars, had a house in Wigford by 1269. By 1315 the order had 40 friars in Lincoln. A house of Austin Friars stood on the north side of Rasen Lane in Newport and the Friars of the Sack had a short-lived house at Stamp End by the river.

The preface 'Concerning the Service of the Church' to the new *Book of Common Prayer* of the Church of England introduced at the beginning of the reign of Elizabeth I referred specifically to Lincoln:

'And whereas heretofore there hath been great diversity in saying and singing in Churches within the Realm: some following Salisbury Use. some Hereford Use. some the Use of Bangor. some of York. some of Lincoln. now from henceforth all the whole Realm shall have but one use.'

By the reign of Henry VIII the divine services of many parish churches and larger churches followed the form of the Latin liturgy used in Salisbury Cathedral, known as the Sarum Use or Rite. Clearly, however, Lincoln had kept its own ancient Use, taken in 1072 from Rouen, although no copy of it survived the Reformation. The authors of the new English *Prayer Book*, in their pursuit of uniformity, regarded the Lincoln Rite as one more confusing anomaly to be suppressed. The new rite was to be in the common tongue instead of in Latin.

However, the Henrician Reformation was not at first or simply about replacing a diversity of Latin Uses with a uniform English rite. In 1509, the year Henry became King, Thomas Wolsey was made Dean of Lincoln and then, in 1514, Bishop. In the following year Wolsey was translated to York and received a cardinal's hat, in honour of which the former Cardinal's Hat inn still stands at the top of the High Street. When he was made Lord Chancellor of England the city continued to look to him as its patron. Wolsey fell from grace because he failed to deliver the King's divorce from Queen Catherine of Aragon. The 'Great Matter' of Henry's divorce touched Lincoln in the summer of 1534, when every citizen from the highest to the lowest swore allegiance to the offspring of Henry and Anne Boleyn and repudiated all foreign authority (*ie*: the Pope). That autumn, fearing an uprising, the King ordered an inspection of the arms and armour held within the city. Five months later Henry was proclaimed Supreme Head of the Church of England at the Stonebow and at St Mary-le-Wigford. Henceforth all references to the bishop of Rome were to be removed from the service books of the Church.

Events were moving fast. Later that year the Royal commissioners reached Lincolnshire and began dissolving the smaller monasteries. This was the signal for the looked-for uprising and, when the harvest was in, the people of the Wolds market towns and villages were up in arms under their captains, compelling as many gentlemen as they could lay hands on to accompany them as their born spokesmen. The precursor of the better-known Pilgrimage of Grace, the Lincolnshire Rising of 1536 was a well-organised attempt to oblige the King to remove those unpopular ministers who were turning him against his loyal subjects. The rebels' leaders were tradesmen and craftsmen. They marched on Lincoln in their militia companies wapentake by wapentake, a disciplined force, reportedly 40,000 strong, and reached Lincoln on the evening of Friday 6 October, where an advance party had been sent to prepare lodgings. Somehow room was found for 25,000 in the city, increasing its population fourfold. The rest were lodged outside. The evidence taken after the Rising had collapsed shows that the Mayor of Lincoln and the Dean had been hostile to the rebels and the Mayor had been ordered to hold the city against them. On the other hand some of the Cathedral canons were clearly sympathetic to their cause.

While the commons assembled on Newport Green, the gentry held a council at Mile Cross on the outskirts of the city, at which articles containing their demands were drawn up to be sent to the King. On the following day, when they were met in the Chapter House of the Cathedral, the rebels were encouraged by news that Beverley and Halifax had also risen. Meanwhile, the intelligence reaching the King in London was inaccurate, confusing and alarming. He was said to be in great fear. Indeed it was not until several days after the rebels arrived in Lincoln that Royal forces took the field. Instead, on Tuesday 10 October a Royal messenger arrived at the chapter house, escorted by 300 rebels, bearing a letter from the King, containing a sentence which has gone down in Lincolnshire history. After ordering the rebels to hand over their leaders and go home, the King continued:

'How presumptious then, are ye, the rude commons of one shire, and that one of the most brute and beastly of the whole realm, and of least experience, to take upon you, contrary to God's law and man's law, to rule your prince whom you are bound to obey and serve and for no worldly cause to withstand.'

Not surprisingly, when he came to read these words to the assembled commons, Thomas Moigne of Willingham deemed it prudent to omit them, but his hesitation aroused the suspicion that some treachery was on foot. The commons withdrew to the cloisters and agreed to waylay Moigne and kill him as he went out of the west door of the Cathedral, but he was warned and, leaving by the south door, took refuge in the Chancellor's house.

However, by now some of the rebels had begun to lose heart, fearing the approach of the King's forces. Lancaster Herald arrived in Lincoln and, on Thursday 12 October, issued a Royal proclamation to all men to submit and go home. Nevertheless, it was not until the following Tuesday that the forces of the King under the Duke of Suffolk, the leading Lincolnshire landowner, finally entered Lincoln. The gentlemen who had taken part in the rising were arrested, and five months later were tried, found guilty of high treason and executed at Lincoln.

It had been a close-run thing for the Tudor dynasty, but now the work of dissolving the thirteen remaining religious houses in the city could go forward without hindrance. There was no resistance and it was soon over, with few regrets. The first to be surrendered to the agents of Thomas Cromwell was the Gilbertine Priory of St Katherine. Its canons were pensioned off but the nuns received nothing. Seven months later, in February 1539, the four houses of friars were dissolved. Later in the year the small and little-used Benedictine house of St Mary Magdalene, belonging to the Abbey of St Mary at York, was abandoned, its existence now recalled by a few ruins south of Monks Road. The property of these city-centre religious communities was not great and was leased or purchased by city aldermen or citizens. The land of the Bendictines (the Black monks) was eventually incorporated into the common land of the city. In the nineteenth century this Monks Leys Common became a park called the Arboretum. Richer pickings were to be had from the property which nearly fifty monasteries or convents outside Lincoln owned within the city before the dissolution, amounting to an estimated third of the property in city and suburbs. Once considered to be land 'in mortmain' (in the 'dead hand' of the Church, ie: for eternity) all this property was now released as freehold and made the Duke of Suffolk one of the principal landlords.

The resistance shown by the Dean of Lincoln to the rebels does not seem to have much influenced the agents of Henry VIII when they reached Lincoln in quest of 'shrynes and other jewels' to be seized in 1542. The shrine of St Hugh's body ('with which all simple people be much deceived and brought into great superstition and idolatry') was broken up so that nothing remained, and the precious metals and jewels were taken for the King. Hugh's bones are said to have been reburied in the retro-choir on the spot now marked by a 17th century table tomb. At the same time relics, chalices, plate, jewels from the Bishop's mitre, and hundreds of vestments were carried off to the Jewel House in the Tower of London — in all 2,621 ounces of gold and 4,285 ounces of silver. Watching as the Cathedral was plundered, the Treasurer cast his keys to the ground and strode out of the building saying 'Ceasing the treasure, so ceaseth the office of treasurer'. Perhaps the particularly complete destruction of Hugh's shrine was motivated by his fearless defence of the rights and privileges of the Church against Royal interference — not a model which Henry VIII wished bishops to emulate. A few years later, masses for the departed were abolished and the chantry chapels where they were offered were dissolved. The city properties with which these chantries were endowed were confiscated and sold to various gentlemen. The chantry of Bishop Longland, Henry VIII's confessor and a target of the rebels' anger in the Lincolnshire Rising, was left in its unfinished state east of the south choir transept of the Cathedral, his only memorial being, says the punning inscription, the measure of land God gave him for his tomb, ('Longa terra mensura eius Dominus dedit'). Nevertheless the old ways died hard. Even in Queen Elizabeth's time Lincolnshire folk persisted in bequeathing money to the 'Mother Church of Lincoln' just as their forebears did before the Reformation.

When John Leland came to Lincoln on his peregrination of the Kingdom he claimed to have seen thirty-eight churches. By 1549 only nine remained. In 1553 the Bishop and Mayor were authorised to unite the churches in the city, Bail, and Close into fifteen parishes. After closure the Common Council had the right to the materials. The stone of redundant churches was used to repair roads or for the retaining wall of the Brayford Pool. In 1559 the tiles of St John-le-Wigford were reused in a house belonging to the city, the chancel and choir were granted to the Mayor and his brother, and the steeple was all that was left standing.

ABOVE: Site of the Malandry of the Holy Innocents, the leper hospital, on the edge of the South Common, safely outside the city walls. OPPOSITE LEFT: The pre-Conquest tower of St Mary-le-Wigford, Lincoln. RIGHT: St Peter-at-Gowts, another typical Lincoln pre-Conquest tower. BELOW: The churchyard of St Michael-on-the-Mount, a medieval church rebuilt in the nineteenth century, which now serves the students of the Theological College and their families.

65

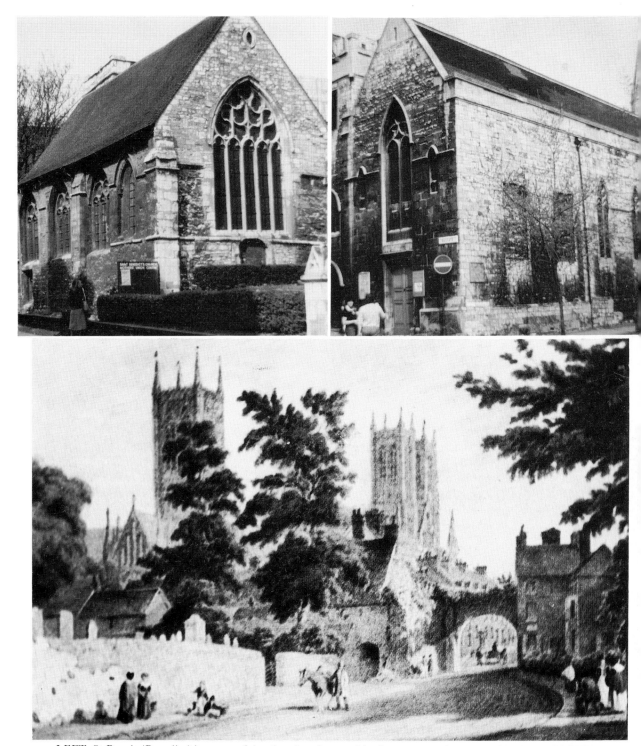

LEFT: St Bene't (Benedict's) — one of the churches damaged in the seventeenth century Civil War. RIGHT: St Mary Magdalen, built to serve the parishioners whose worship in the Morning Chapel of the cathedral disturbed the canons. BELOW: St John-in-Newport, now demolished, formerly served the suburb which grew up after the castle was built.

ABOVE LEFT: The churchyard of St John-in-Newport today. Gravestones recall the farming community of 150 years ago. RIGHT: St Mary's 'abbey', more accurately a tiny cell of St Mary's, York. Rarely occupied, at the Reformation the estates became the Monks Leys. BELOW LEFT: Whitefriars — the late fifteenth century timber-framed convent of the Carmelites, now visible from Tentercroft Street carpark. RIGHT: Greyfriars — the convent of the Franciscans who came to Lincoln at the behest of Bishop Grosseteste.

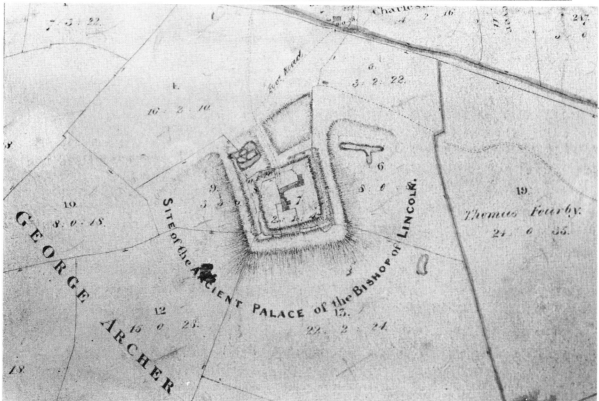

ABOVE: The hall of St Mary's Guild, in the wealthy suburb of the Wigford, founded by St Hugh to raise funds for the Cathedral fabric. BELOW: The medieval bishops used several residences as each in turn became foul and in need of airing. St Hugh was often at Stow and his pet swan lived on the moat.

The Moneymen

Around the central core of the city lay a number of suburbs (perhaps the equivalents of the 'faubourgs' of French cities of the time). Such was the Newport, or new market, which had grown up on the north side of the city after the building of the Castle. Here in the middle ages a ribbon of long narrow building plots backed onto the open common fields either side of the High Street, or Newport Green, up to the Kings Ditch on the east. Some of the wealthiest citizens lived outside the walls of the lower city in the suburb of Wigford, extending south for a mile along Ermine Street. Here, St Mary's Guildhall, sometimes referred to locally as 'John of Gaunt's Stables', with its splendid, ornately carved, Romanesque main gate, is a fine example of twelfth century secular building, built between 1170 and 1180 for one of the most important religious gilds in the city. Used until recently as a timber store, the guildhall is a splendid monument to the prosperity of Lincoln in late Norman times. It was built directly on the carriageway of the Roman Fosse Way, over which the building line had by that date encroached. Originally taller with a first floor hall, its height was reduced in the seventeenth century.

Norman features also occur in houses along James Street, while other fine stone buildings have been revealed by excavation on Friars Lane, east of Broadgate in the area of the former suburb called the Butwerk, originally considered to have been a rather poor part of the city and in Flaxengate and Michaelgate. Another fine Norman building, to judge from surviving illustrations, was St Andrew's Hall, which was demolished in the eighteenth century. Like St Mary's Hall, it stood in the Wigford, further evidence of the great prosperity of this suburb in the twelfth century, when excavation shows that stone was replacing timber.

Much is now known about many of the houses built before 1500 in uphill Lincoln, as a result of a survey carried out since 1970. Many of these witness to the enormous increase and elaboration of the Cathedral establishment in the twelfth and thirteenth centuries. At first the Cathedral canons had to find houses for themselves in the uphill parishes. Not until 1160 was the Subdean given a house attached to his office, on the south side of the Minster. Others followed. The Deans lived on the north side from about 1184 until 1960 when they too moved to the south side. The Precentor acquired his own house about 1270. However, it was not until the early fourteenth century that the chapter began to buy up property around the Cathedral for the canons' use. At the same time houses were demolished to make way for a wall enclosing the land around the Cathedral. This close wall was completed by 1328.

Since the middle years of the fifteenth century, however, much Dean and Chapter property has been leased to lay people, in some families for generations. Often, but not always, the leaseholders, especially in the houses in the Close, have had some connection with the Cathedral, such as clerks of the works or surveyors. The great Elizabethan composer William Byrd, who was choirmaster at Lincoln, lived in a house on the site of number six, The Close. There were also MPs, judges, gentry, a dancing master, even a future Governor of pre-Revolutionary Massachusetts, among the Dean and Chapter leaseholders. The Dean and Chapter houses on Steep Hill, the Strait, down the High Street and along Waterside, however, tended to be occupied by well-to-do tradesmen.

One of the most impressive of these ancient houses is The Chancery, residence of the Chancellors of the Cathedral since 1321 when Anthony Bek, a rather domineering Chancellor, was given the property because he wanted a bigger house. Before that the rent had been put towards the completion of St Hugh's Shrine and afterwards into the Cathedral fabric fund. In 1390 the house acquired its most celebrated tenant in the person of Katherine Swynford, the love of 'old John of Gaunt, time-honoured Lancaster' who, in 1397, obtained a Papal dispensation to marry her. He came to Lincoln and they were married in the Minster after the Octave of the Epiphany 1397. The private chapel, great chamber, and solar were there in Katherine's day but the brick frontage is a century later, and may have been built by workmen employed by Bishop Thomas Rotherham on the Bishop's palace at Buckden, using the same style of brick with stone dressing. The hall with its central hearth was demolished in 1714.

In sharp contrast is the row of small houses on Greestone Terrace. In the mid-seventeenth century one was lived in by 'a very poor man ... who sweepeth the church'. Another was occupied by 'a poore widow one of the sweepers of the church ...'. The choirboys lived in a house on Pottergate (number ten), 'an ancient vast building' with an open hall, which was rebuilt in 1661 to accommodate the choristers, sterward, and singing master. The twenty-five senior vicars choral, that is the clergy who, from St Hugh's time, sang the offices in choir in place of the non-resident canons, lived in Vicars' Court, the building of which was begun in the late thirteenth century, on the south side of the Cathedral on a plot of land called the Boungarth.

Beyond Vicars' Court are the remains of the Palace where the medieval bishops of Lincoln held court. The first bishops seem to have occupied chambers over the Roman East Gate. King Stephen gave land near St Michael's Church for Bishop Alexander to build himself a dwelling, but nothing seems to have happened, because twenty years later Henry II granted Bishop Robert de Chesney an adjacent piece of land abutting on the Roman walls. It was said that the land was obtained at great expense. By 1163 it seems that the Bishop's house had been built, but little more than twenty years later St Hugh began to build a more magnificent aisled hall to the west of Bishop de Chesney's hall. This new work was completed by Bishop Hugh de Welles, using stone quarried from the town ditch and timber from Sherwood Forest. Just over a century later, Bishop Henry Burghersh received a Royal licence to crenellate, that is to add battlements and turrets to his residence and walls, more for prestige than for actual defence. At the same time the Bishop was allowed to insert a new gate in the north-east corner of the wall at the point where the entrance to the palace grounds through a Victorian arch is today.

A fifteenth century bishop, William Alnwick, added the great gate tower which bears his name, a chapel range, and made other improvements. However, within less than a century, the Palace had become seriously dilapidated. Damaged in the occupation of the Close during the Lincolnshire Rising of 1536, it was nevertheless fit for Henry VIII and Queen Catherine Howard to stay, as guests of Bishop Longland in 1541 and their coat of arms was set up to commemorate their visit. James I was received at the Palace by Bishop Neile in 1617 and Bishop Williams undertook major repairs during his episcopate (1621–41), to the extent of installing an extensive library. During the rebuilding, Bishop Williams lived in the Bishop's Palace at Buckden in Huntingdonshire, and this remained the usual residence of the Bishops of Lincoln during the Civil War and up to the nineteenth century.

The oldest houses still standing in the city are those associated in popular lore with the Jewish community of Lincoln, notably the Jews House and the house which has traditionally been attributed to Aaron, the Jew of Lincoln, but which was described in the thirteenth century as belonging to Peter of Legbourne and his wife. The so-called Jews' houses are evidence of the strength of the merchant community of Lincoln in the twelfth century. There had been a Jewish community in Lincoln since 1159. Of 748 English Jews whose names are known, 82 were of Lincoln, making this one of the largest communities in England. Strongly built of stone, at a time when mainly churches and civic buildings were of stone, with Norman or Romanesque doorways and windows, these houses stand on the street that is called The Strait, leading up to the Bail or outer bailey of the Castle. Under Henry I Jews and their possessions were the property of the King. Wherever the Jews settled, the King's subjects were obliged to protect them. However, so unreliable was this considered that the Jews of Lincoln lived, not in a Jewry or ghetto, but close under the Royal Castle in order, if danger threatened, that they could be got quickly to safety within its walls. Indeed, in 1189, inflamed by the call to the Third Crusade (and the rumour that Richard the Lion Heart had ordered the extermination of the Jews), mobs in various English cities turned on them, accusing them of the murder of Christ.

The Jews of Lincoln cannot fail to have heard of how the Jews of York, little more than a day's journey from Lincoln, threatened by a furious mob, had barricaded themselves in Clifford's Tower and, in an act recalling the last stand against the Romans at Masada, had taken their own lives rather than fall into the hands of their attackers. Even those Jews who offered to convert to Christianity in return for their lives were put to death by the people of York and their corpses left unburied in the streets. In Lincoln the leading figures among the townspeople instigated an anti-Jewish riot and a crowd attacked the Cathedral, where the bonds recording the debts owing to Jewish merchant bankers were held for safe-keeping. However, St Hugh himself alone faced the mob down and saved the Jews from the fate of their brothers and sisters at York.

It is conceivable that the privileged position Jews held was partly responsible for racial hatred. The Jews had a larger measure of freedom than other citizens of Lincoln. Moreover, the popular teaching of the Church, blaming the Jews for the death of Christ, was an important factor in this anti-semitism and could be used to whip up the mob. It underlay the claim that, at the Passover Feast in 1255 (which occurs near the Christian Easter festival) Jews from all over England had come to Lincoln for the sacrifice of a Christian boy, Hugh by name, from the Dernstall, in a mock crucifixion, in order to use his blood to bake matzot, unleavened bread. The child's body, it was claimed, was discovered by the authorities in a well in the house of Jopin. Jopin turned King's evidence and incriminated over 90 of his fellows, who had come to Lincoln for a wedding.

This story of the ritual murder (the Blood Libel) of 'yonge Hugh of Lyncoln' was repeated in many versions (and was still going strong when Chaucer included it in his *Canterbury Tales* almost a century after the Jews had been expelled from England). Similar racist tales are found at Norwich (where it may have been concocted by the Church), Gloucester and Bristol, and as recently as the 1940s, in Poland. Although refuted by several churchmen, this did not stop eighteen Jews being executed for the supposed crime and did not prevent the canons from setting up, in the south choir transept of the Cathedral, a shrine to 'Little *Saint* Hugh'. Today the remains of this shrine remind us of this shameful episode in the ancient history of racial prejudice.

Forty years earlier, the Jews of Lincoln had been subjected to a decree by a Council of the Church which, calling Jews the blasphemers of Christ, set them apart from their Christian neighbours by their dress, barred them from public office (and hence authority over Christians), and from marriage with Christians. This Council also attempted to restrict Jews in their practice of one of the few professions open to them, that of banking.

The commercial life of cities like Lincoln could not have expanded without credit. However, the teaching of the medieval Church, based on St Luke's Gospel (Chap 6 *v* 35) prohibited Christians from charging interest. The frequency with which the Church ruled upon this implies that its teaching was honoured in the breach. However, Jews were not included in this prohibition. Indeed, the Hebrew Bible (notably the Books of Exodus and Deuteronomy) allows interest to be charged on loans to non-Jews. The Church made it difficult for the Christian businessmen of medieval Lincoln to charge interest. Hence, since the early twelfth century, the Jews of Lincoln had supplied an essential service as its bankers, supplying the loans, mortgages, and overdrafts needed to make the wheels of business turn.

One of the most prominent of the Jewish financial houses was that of Aaron of Lincoln (c1125–1186), the wealthiest Jew, and possibly the richest man in the whole of twelfth century Europe. His financial activities extended throughout the kingdom, from Cumberland to Kent. People in need of money, for instance to pay legal fees, to raise money for a crusading expedition, or even to pay the King's subsidy, turned to him. The Dean and Chapter of Lincoln borrowed from Aaron (for building work on the Minster), as did at least eleven Abbeys, including those of St Albans and Peterborough. So too did King Henry II. However, the majority of Aaron's clients were small landowners who mortgaged their estates to him. Increasingly they found themselves over-extended and unable to repay the money they had borrowed and their lands became forfeit to Aaron. When Aaron died, the King took over all his affairs. As Aaron and his possessions belonged to the King, all the cash and bullion were confiscated and sent direct to France to finance Henry II's war against his sons, but the ship carrying the treasure sank in the Channel. A separate department with two treasurers and two clerks, 'the exchequer of Aaron', was set up to deal with the rest of his assets, equal to three quarters of the annual income of the King, owed to Aaron of Lincoln by 430 debtors, including the King of Scotland and the Archbishop of Canterbury. Twenty years later some of these debts were still owing and Aaron's son, Elias, was still trying to regain control of his father's estate.

In the mid-thirteenth century, life grew still harder for the Jews, as their usefulness as money-lenders was challenged by Christian dealers, who found a variety of ways to evade the laws of the Church in order to charge interest on loans. Bishop Grosseteste of Lincoln, unlike his saintly predecessor Hugh, saw it as his Christian duty to apply the full rigour of the law against the Jews. Some Lincoln Jews, such as Roger fitz Benedict, three times Mayor and founder of a chantry in the Church of St Peter-in-Eastgate, were converted to Christianity and baptised and the Hospital of St Bartholomew outside Lincoln is said to have been used for converts. In the year in which Edward I expelled the Jews from England, a Lincoln Jewess, Bellaset from Wallingford in Oxfordshire, was executed for uttering counterfeit coin.

The inhabited area had begun to contract even before the end of the fourteenth century and many houses were in ruins. The inquest on the death of Walter de Poynton of Canwick in 1367 referred to three of his fourteen messuages, which had stood empty and without tenants for three years, and to other property, including a cottage and four small shops which were also standing empty. Nine years after this the King committed a garden and two ruinous plots in the parish of St Michael-on-the-Mount and two ruinous plots in St Bavons to Walter de Askeby. In 1428 four city parishes had no inhabitants, while seventeen had not more than ten persons in them. In 1466 the King made a number of concessions to the city on the grounds of its desolation and decay, the ruin of houses and 'the poverty and paucity of its inhabitants'. Certain taxes were remitted and some messuages belonging to the King, one of which was said to be 'weak and ruinous', were granted to the citizens. Several houses belonging to the Cathedral Chapter also stood empty or were dilapidated. It seems likely that, on the eve of the Tudor period, Lincoln had become a one-street town of 400 houses. At the beginning of Elizabeth I's reign, the city authorities were obliged to order that no more houses be pulled down. The income from the 'land toll penny' in the mid-sixteenth century suggests a population of about 2,000, and eight or nine parts of the city were said to be 'clean fallen to ruin'.

The archaeological record bears out the written testimony. The investigation of sites near the central spine of the medieval city shows that the decline of Lincoln was no exaggeration cooked up to obtain fiscal advantages for the citizens. The once thriving Flaxengate site was largely derelict by the sixteenth century. Part of the Grantham Street site was in a similar condition and remained vacant until the building of a terrace of houses three centuries later. On the corner where Flaxengate turns into Danes Terrace, a house had been steadily pulled down since the fourteenth century until only a section was still standing. With so many deserted plots, and houses and churches falling into ruin, Lincoln's medieval heyday was followed, as its Roman splendour had been, by a new dark age.

Examples from more than a hundred probate inventories provide a glimpse of the plans and interiors of small houses in Elizabethan Lincoln, most of them still within the medieval building tradition. Elizabeth Clarkson's house in 1574 consisted of the best parlour, containing beds, a chest, and a chair of wainscot, the hall furnished with a table, a boarded chair, a cupboard, a latten basin and ewer, the buttery, the lower parlour, best parlour, the chamber over the kitchen, the chamber over the hall, chamber over the best parlour, and the high chamber. The high chamber suggests a three storeyed house. In the same year the house which Thomas Dent, a founder leased, consisted of the hall, containing platters, dishes, fireside implements, a wool wheel (and, unusually, window glass), kitchen, chamber, parlour and shop. The house leased by William Tindale, skinner, in 1575 had a hall, chamber over the hall, another chamber, shop, chamber over the far shop, chamber above, a brewhouse and two stables. He also leased a house in Newland. The interior of the first floor of the Wig and Mitre on the Strait shows the typical vernacular building materials used in houses like those described in the inventories.

The Bishops' Palace had become derelict by the seventeenth century Civil War, when it was further damaged. Thereafter, the bishops lived mainly at Buckden on the Great North Road in Northamptonshire.

ABOVE: This prebendal house has been occupied at different times by the Subdean and Dean. BELOW: The Chancery, occupied by the Chancellors of Lincoln since 1321. OPPOSITE ABOVE: The rear of the Chancery as it might have looked when Katherine Swynford lived here, before she married John of Gaunt. BELOW: An imaginative reconstruction of another large medieval house in Minster Yard.

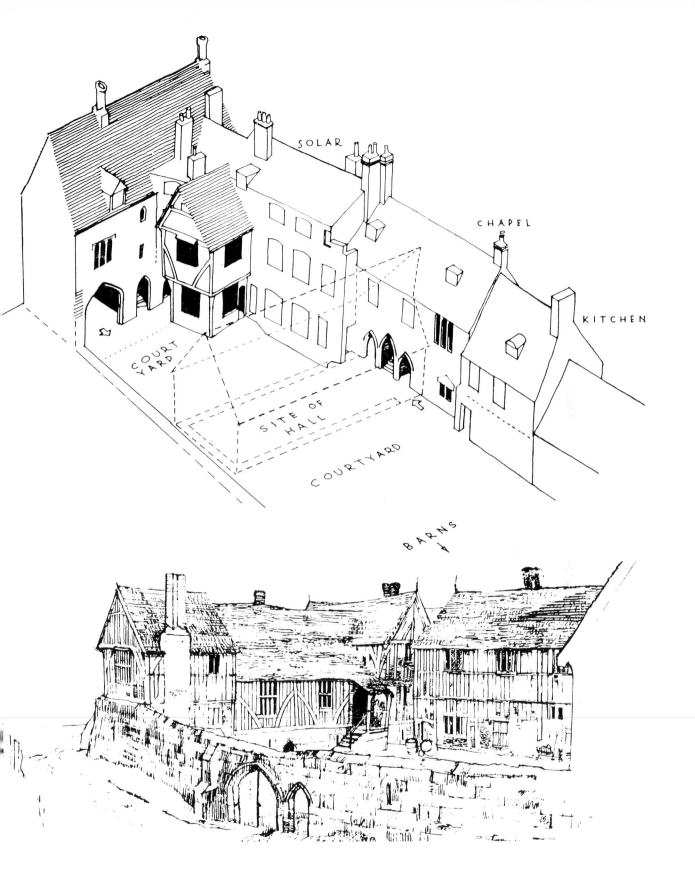

SOLAR

CHAPEL

KITCHEN

COURT YARD

SITE OF HALL

COURTYARD

BARNS

ABOVE: In the foreground a former inn, and beyond it The Rest — a timber-framed medieval house. LEFT: A substantial timber-framed late-medieval house in the Bail before restoration and RIGHT: after.

Pestilence, Famine and War

In the century between the upheavals of the Henrician Reformation and the outbreak of the Civil War, one is hard pressed to find evidence from Lincoln of any late Tudor flowering of English literature, art, and music. No such renaissance was experienced. It is true that one of the greatest English composers, William Byrd, the English Palestrina, was for a brief time organist and choirmaster of the Cathedral and resided in a house on the site of no 6, Minster Yard. Born in 1543 (two years before the death of another great Lincolnshire composer of Tudor church music, John Taverner, at Boston), it is thought in Lincoln, he was a pupil of Thomas Tallis. At the age of twenty he was appointed organist and master of the choristers, regardless of his adherence to the old faith, and in the next seven years so established his reputation as a composer in a variety of styles that, in spite of his recusancy, he was sworn a Gentleman of the Chapel Royal and in 1572 moved to London, although the Cathedral authorities continued to pay him to produce music for them on special occasions. Byrd is the Shakespeare of English music, and his wonderful music affords evidence of the quality of the choir at Lincoln in these years, notwithstanding the depredations recently wrought on the Minster and the changes in the worship of the church by which the Lincoln Use had been suppressed.

The ancient Use of the Cathedral were not the only customs to have been suppressed at the Reformation. The annual cycle of plays came under the prohibition of festivals and holy days. Although in 1554 and 1555, during the brief Catholic restoration under Mary Tudor, the Corporation ordered 'St Anne's Gild with the Corpus Christi play' to be brought out again, ten years later, in place of the Biblical Cycle, 'a standing play' of Old Tobit was put on, using an array of traditional props kept in St Swithun's Church. The City Waits were summoned to Grimsthorpe to perform before the Duchess of Suffolk at the Twelfth Night festivities in 1561 and again in 1562.

Even so, much of the pageantry had gone out of civic life. Rather the Elizabethan years were times of plague, poverty and want in Lincoln. In the city the price of the foodstuffs (beans, oats, barley, rye) which formed the basic diet of the poor had been rising since the 1540s, creating great hardship. Beggars were coming to town, constituting a threat to stability. This was a period which saw the introduction by Tudor governments of a series of measures to deal with the growing problem of poverty by singling out the able-bodied and indigent poor (the sturdy beggars) for special treatment. A pillory had been set up in St Benedict's parish — next the constables were to bring all unauthorised beggars and vagrants in front of the Mayor; later all authorised beggars were made to wear badges. The city was divided into wards (a ward in the old sense was a security zone), each one under a team of aldermen to catch and punish vagabonds and put young people to work.

In 1551 an attempt was made to create jobs by establishing a cloth mill and dyehouse. Anyone who refused to work in the new undertaking was to have a month's notice to leave the city. There was, unsurprisingly, some friction between the new clothiers and the ancient gild of weavers. On the other hand, the Lincoln clothiers were helped by a Royal licence to buy and sell wool throughout the county. Nevertheless the undertaking does not seem to have made much progress. A little later the Mayor and Sheriffs donated part of their official salaries towards a fund to provide starter loans to help young craftsmen set themselves up in business. Corn continued in short supply and prices continued to rise sharply. Distress among the poor increased in like measure and the nature of the government's intervention changed from encouraging voluntary action to enforcement. The 'beadle of the beggars' is heard of in 1560 and, by the end of the sixteenth century, the 'Old' or Elizabethan Poor Law had established the compulsory poor rate collected on a parish basis. The 'master of the poor' was paid to expel all those without visible means of support who had not been born in Lincoln or lived three years there. An earlier project for a house of industry was reintroduced and in 1596 a room under the former Grey Friars building became a jersey knitting and spinning shop, run by a true Jerseyman, William Marett.

As was the case elsewhere, private charity afforded some measure of relief for the poverty-stricken of the city. From 1566 to 1653 seven bequests provided endowments to help the poor, totalling more than £1,140, mainly arising from the rents of property left to the Corporation. The money was distributed either to the poor without discrimination, specifically to the poor of St Swithin's and St Peter-in-Eastgate parishes, to four widows, in order to apprentice poor children born in the city but of freemen, or as loans to young men, freemen by birth and inhabitants of the city, to help them start in trade, preferably as clothiers.

Further pressure was put on the city's stretched resources by outbreaks of plague. In 1550 and again in 1557 and '58 the sick were confined to their houses to prevent the spread of disease and a subscription raised for their support. Plague returned in the summer of 1586 but, with the failure of the harvest and serious flooding, the city was invaded by poor people seeking relief and it became necessary to enforce the by-laws concerning residence, to prevent the influx of beggars. From Holy Rood Day 1586 to the same day a year later five Mayors had to be elected because of deaths. Plague again ravaged the city in 1590 and 1599. It seems to have made its last visitation between July 1630 and August 1632. St Lawrence's Church was called the 'pest' church. St Margaret's register records 41 burials between 25 July 1631 'when the sickness began in this parish' to 4 December ('the last that died of sickness'). From 1542 to 1715 (except for 1566–1615) the burials recorded in the registers of St Peter-at-Gowts, a parish in an unhealthy lowlying area, exceeded baptisms.

Efforts to revive Lincoln as a cloth town in the second half of the sixteenth century proved relatively unsuccessful, although there were still a few working clothiers left. Another piece of legislation handed down from the busy Tudor Parliaments, the Statute of Artificers of 1563, set up the annual State or 'hiring' fairs, whereby all unemployed servants and workmen had to attend at the Stonebow to hire themselves for a year to a master and take the hiring or 'fezzin'' penny to fasten the contract. This went on until this century. Wages were to be fixed by the JPs in accordance with the prices of grain and victuals. The same statute also required the city authorities to undertake an overhaul of gild and company charters. The trade and craft gilds had also suffered a reduction of their influence during the Reformation, as a result of the suppression of their spiritual functions and the confiscation of their religious endowments.

Thirty-five crafts were represented in the apprenticeship records of the early Tudor city but some trades, such as the building trades and the various types of metalworkers, were not organised in gilds and had been combined into companies. Some apprentices came from as far afield as Westmoreland, Cumberland, and Yorkshire. In particular, city boys were not interested in glove-making because most apprentices in this trade came from over twenty-five miles away. Although the law barred husbandmen from entering a trade, some Lincoln apprentices had been husbandmen. The law also required a seven years' apprenticeship, but some Lincoln apprentices served a shorter time while others served twice as long. The Elizabethan Corporation tightened up the ancient rules governing apprenticeship and monopoly. The new rules meant that new apprentices had to be enrolled before the Mayor. The number of enrolments in each craft suggest that the leather and metal-working trades in the city were in quite good shape, as were the clothing and food trades. However, the building trades and cloth manufacturing trades were at a low ebb with few apprentices enrolled.

Notwithstanding considerable efforts in 1521 to clear the Foss Dyke, when the Mayor laid out £17 of his own money to keep men on work, and Hull and York were asked to make a financial contribution, more work was needed in 1522. In 1529 and 1530 landowners along the canal were required to maintain their banks and clear sedge. Nevertheless complaints were heard in 1571 that timber, thatch, and turf were too expensive, due to the difficulty of carrying them by water, and the Corporation promoted an Act of Parliament which would have allowed it to levy a rate on everyone within a seven-mile radius to scour the Foss Dyke. In 1597, as part of the programme to encourage the city economy, five citizens were commanded to arrange the purchase of the lease of St John's churchyard 'and dispose of it to such good purpose for the commodity of the city, by falling the steeple, walling the ground, and paving, as shall seem best. Ordered that the Cornmarket be kept there, except for oats and ground meal which are to be sold as before on the Old Hill' by St Mary-le-Wigford churchyard wall.

Street names from the period include Tolbothe Lane east of the Stone(Stan)bow; Briggate from the Stonebow to the High Bridge; and Micklegate above Stonebow to the Strait. Notwithstanding its poverty, the city enjoyed the benefits of the water supply provided by St Mary's Conduit ('the new castell of the conduit' as Leland called it). Constructed by the Blackfriars, it was fed by a spring on the hill to the east of Lincoln near Monks Lane, from which pipes led to several conduits. Another legacy of the pre-Reformation Church found a new use in 1558, when Mr Justice Monson gave the old Grey Friars building to the Corporation for the foundation of a grammar school, which occupied the chapel on the upper floor.

In 1583, encouraged by the Bishop, who had been a master, the Cathedral School for the 'chanters' was combined with the grammar school, the Dean and residentiary canons appointing the master of the upper school and the Mayor, the recorder and five aldermen having the appointment of the usher in the lower school. The new foundation stood in Goldsmith Alley. In 1673 it was recalled that there had formerly belonged to these schools 'a great number of books in two presses for the use of the scholars but now they are for the most part by tradition worn out or pilfered in the time of the War'. In 1602, by the will of Richard Smith, an estate at Potter Hanworth was left to establish a Blue Coat or Christ's Hospital School for twelve poor boys from Lincoln, Potter Hanworth, or Welton, to be educated until they were fourteen or fifteen and then to be apprenticed.

It was a city of gardens and orchards. Alderman Richard Somerby's will in 1644 left his property, called Grangershouse, in the parish of St Peter-at-Arches with the piece of land adjoining, a plot of ground, a cottage in Newland which he had recently built with 'the ground called gardenstead' and a plot of land adjoining, leading into Newland, being a convenient passage into Newland. Elsewhere Mrs Ryther allowed Sir Thomas Meers to wall up the door of a passage to the Bail between her orchard and his orchard, so that the doorstead 'be made a sort of small convenience for spades a foot wide'. The fields came right up to the city. In 1724 the Dean and Chapter leased six oxgangs of land in the fields of Lincoln, together with the manor house in Newport, to Ann Ball. North of this, according to another lease sixty years earlier was the Pinfold, together with a cottage, a beasthouse, barn, and yard. References to Newport Close, Dalderby (or Tower) Close, and other closes show that some piecemeal enclosure of the open and common fields had already begun in the later years of the seventeenth century. A sale of sixty-two acres in 1659 included a four acre close of pasture, together with thirty-four acres of arable, ten acres of meadow, and six acres of pasture in Newport, plus eight acres of arable in the fields of the city and meadow in Long Leas. In 1800 two cottages in Newport were advertised for sale, with right of common on the Carholm or West Common. At that time the city was bounded by hedges to south and north.

Some open space was the result of the Civil War. In 1649, the year the King was beheaded, the widow of Dr John Farmery sold the ground where his house had stood 'but now utterly demolished or destroyed'. This, too, was where most of the fighting had taken place in 1644. The derelict Palace of the medieval bishops was one of the buildings which suffered. Already damaged and with the lead from the roof plundered, it was set on fire by Royalist troops during the so-called second Civil War in 1648 and was left an open shell, its stone used as a quarry for repairs to the Cathedral. However, it was claimed that those who laid hands on the lead and stone from the Bishop's Palace suffered untimely ends. Philip Clark, the labourer that carried the lead, broke his neck as he went down the hill. John Peachy, the plumber that cast the lead, slipped into the pit and was scalded to death. Mr Tooley of Boston, who sent the lead to Amsterdam, sunk it in sight of the harbour and lost it. Squire Whichcote and his son took the stone to build a house at Harpswell but died before the walls were six feet high.

A glance at the list of the seventy-five persons in the city who, in July 1642, promised horses and men for the King shows unsurprisingly that his support came largely from the uphill clergy and gentry living round the Cathedral. (In 1631 the Bishop of Lincoln had been presented for having a play in his house on the Lord's Day.) When Charles I visited Lincoln in person on 12 July 1642 he was given a rapturous welcome by 60,000 people, to the discomfort of the supporters of Parliament, who had believed the city to be on their side.

However, Lincoln suffered by being caught between the Royalist stronghold in Newark-on-Trent to the south-west and the Parliamentary stronghold in Hull to the north. Control of the city swung first to one side, then to the other. Thus by February 1643, Lincoln was controlled by the forces of Parliament. In April Royalist cavalry from the Newark garrison appeared below the city walls but without effect. In the same month Oliver Cromwell and Sir John Hotham spent a week at Lincoln before moving to Nottingham. A further Royalist attempt on Lincoln was made by troops from the Gainsborough garrison. In July 1643, after the fall of Gainsborough, Lord Willoughby of Parham, the commander of the Parliament army in Lincolnshire, fell back to Lincoln before the advance of the army of the Earl of Newcastle, then abandoned the city in his headlong retreat to Boston. A Royalist garrison then occupied Lincoln but surrendered to the Earl of Manchester after the Parliamentary victory at Winceby Field in October 1643.

The city was now occupied by one of the crack regiments of the Eastern Association. However, in March 1644, Lincoln was again abandoned to the Royalists when, having relieved Newark, Prince Rupert threatened to lay siege. Finally, on 3 May 1644, the Earl of Manchester reoccupied the lower city and stormed the Bail three days later, driving the Royalists into the Castle and Cathedral. Manchester's troops took fifteen minutes to fight their way to the Castle ramparts. Under a hail of heavy stones from the parapets, the attackers managed to get ladders up to the walls and, although these were too short, Manchester's men scaled the battlements and routed the Royalist defenders. The Governor, Sir Francis Fane, his officers, and 650 men were taken prisoner. The Earl of Manchester set up his headquarters at the Angel in the Bail while his subordinates gathered in provender and waggons and horses from all over Lincolnshire, in preparation for the campaign that was to end in Parliamentary victory at Marston Moor.

So much damage was done that the Earl of Manchester felt obliged to distribute a dole among the plundered people. The impact of war on an already impoverished city can be imagined. The subdeanery had been sacked and its hall 'pulled down and conveyed away by the soldiers'. Other houses in Minster Yard were demolished 'in the late intestine wars'. St Peter-in-Eastgate and St

Swithun's Churches were destroyed, the latter, it is said, by the explosion of a barrel of gunpowder. St Benedict's and St Mary Magdalene's were badly damaged. St Michael-on-the-Mount had served the Parliament gunners as a target. St John-in-Newport was pulled down in 1649. The bronze effigy on Queen Eleanor of Castile's tomb in the Cathedral was destroyed during the sack of 1644 and the Eleanor Cross on the South Common was smashed in 1648. In common with other castles, it is probable that Lincoln was slighted, that is rendered useless, by order of Parliament.

In June 1648, during the second Civil War, the small parliamentary garrison in Lincoln, faced by a large Royalist force, held out in the Bishop's Palace until compelled to surrender. The Royalists then burned the Palace, leaving it an empty shell. In 1652 it was purchased by one of Cromwell's major-generals, Colonel Berry, as a private house. In 1647 three aldermen were dismissed for having held rank in the King's army. When the monarchy was restored in 1661, seven aldermen, the Sheriffs, a number of common councilmen and the town clerk were removed for having supported Parliament.

LEFT: The Strait, Old English *straete*, meaning a paved street, looking north. RIGHT: The former Cardinal's Hat inn, a much-restored late medieval timber-framed building, named after Cardinal Wolsey.

81

High Town, Low Town

Daniel Defoe was in Lincoln as a government agent in 1712. Writing in 1724, he described Lincoln as 'an ancient, ragged, and still decaying city; it is so full of the ruins of monasteries and religious houses, that, in short, the very barns, stables, outhouses and as they showed me some of the very hog-sties were built church-fashion; that is to say with stone walls and arched windows and doors . . .'. Nevertheless, in the mid-eighteenth century there was evidence of a renaissance. Newspapers were one sign of the development of Lincoln as a provincial capital. In 1728 the *Lincoln Gazette* appeared, followed in 1744 by the *Lincoln Journal*. At the end of the century the *Lincoln Gazetteer* made its appearance but ran for only a year. One of the most celebrated of English provincial newspapers, the *Lincoln, Rutland, and Stamford Mercury*, began publication in Lincoln in 1784. In 1807 the *Hull and Lincolnshire Chronicle* moved to Lincoln. It was printed by the ubiquitous Adam Stark of Gainsborough, historian, postmaster, journalist, and political radical, but closed down in 1810. The master of the Free School had divided his attention between correcting the proofs and correcting his scholars. There was plenty for local papers to report.

After the '45, John Murray, secretary to the rebel army, was sentenced to be a prisoner at large for life and chose Lincoln, where he lived for many years within the liberties of the city. After Culloden, a hundred Jacobite prisoners were brought to Lincoln in four waggons and confined in the Castle. Lincoln was a lively community, especially when its old landmarks were concerned. A plan to remove the spires on the west towers of the Cathedral in 1726 had been frustrated by a mob of 500, assembled, it is said, on a signal given by kicking a football. After two days of protest, the Dean and Chapter had to send a bellman to proclaim that the proposal had been withdrawn — and the Chancellor's beer cellar was emptied on the Cathedral Green. The two spires were eventually taken down in 1808.

Another sign of Georgian revival was the establishment of a theatre. The first one recorded was at the sign of The Harlequin, near the Black Boy on Castle Hill in 1744. It was built by Erasmus Audley, joiner of The Bail, for William Herbert's Company of Comedians and subsequently passed to James Robertson. After 1763 the *mis-en-scène* was moved downhill to the Kings Head in the High Street. William Dibbin wrote in 1788:
'I performed at Lincoln three nights, . . . There is a high town and a low town, and they are as much at variance as the Montagues and the Capulets . . . A playhouse in Lincoln must be in this predicament: if it was situate on the hill, it must be all boxes — if under the hill all gallery and if midway all pit, and as a playhouse cannot live but by box, pit and gallery collectively, I should conceive the last place for the drama in the kingdom is Lincoln.'

The Theatre Royal, Lincoln, was part of a theatrical circuit covered by the Company belonging to Thomas Shaftoe Robertson, otherwise known as 'The Mogul'. He put on plays in Lincoln during Race Week. The advertisement for *Harlequin's Flight to the Gods* in 1795 required an actor to fly 'from the back Part of the Stage to the Top of the Gallery and [a descent] Headforemost over the Pit and . . . A Leap through a Hoop of Daggers'. In 1804, during the French Wars the

ABOVE: More timber-framed late medieval building on the High Bridge
over the River Witham. BELOW: The Glory Hole behind the building on
the High Bridge from the West.

Company performed *The Invasion, or Come If You Dare* and *Cymbeline, King of Britain*. In Race Week 1806 Robertson opened a new Theatre Royal in Lincoln, on the site of St Lawrence's Church, later the city pesthouse, with the Cockpit to the south. The new theatre was influenced by the grandiose new staging of Drury Lane, London. Described as a small brick building, it consisted of pit, two rows of boxes, and a gallery supported by iron columns. The Egyptian influence made popular by the Battle of the Nile was much in evidence and the ceiling was 'a very masterly piece of painting representing a full length figure of Nature'.

In spite of these attractions, theatre in Lincoln was not well supported. *Maria Marten or The Red Barn* was performed there barely two years after the murder it depicted. In 1846 £32 18s 4d was taken by an amateur company for 'the benefit of the declining drama in Lincoln'. The proceeds might have been greater but for £27 spent by the actors and their ladies for wine, gin, rum, brandy, cigars, ale, tobacco, 'six lazy catgut scrapers' and 'oranges for Icilius . . . he whose parching throat did cost 1s.6d.; barber to shave 'em 2s.6d.; tailor to stitch 'em 2s.6d. [and a] footman out of livery 7s.6d.'. In 1858 the bailiffs were in. Actor-manager John Coleman, who occupied the Theatre Royal in the late 19th century for a rent of £15, spoke of fair business in spite of bad weather in Race Week: 'We had no rehearsals, were all young, many of us amiable, and most of us good fellows. We had roaring fires in all parts of the theatre'. At the end of that season, the landlord demanded a further £15 and threatened to lock the stage door but 'I was there as soon as he was, and the result was that he found himself on his back in the snow, while I remained in possession of the theatre'.

On 26 November 1892 the theatre was burnt down, leaving only the walls standing and the dressing room (a more recent part and cut off by an iron door from the rest). A new theatre was opened in 1893 with a performance of *Charley's Aunt*. Designed by Messrs Crewe and Sprague of London and built by Messrs Veale of Stoke Newington, Lincoln's fourth Theatre Royal provided good views, unobstructed by columns, in all parts of the house.

During Race Week the 'quality' of Georgian Lincoln, when it was not at the theatre, congregated at the Assembly Rooms, built in 1744 under the aegis of the Duke of Ancaster, out of money raised by local high society to replace the large, old assembly room at the Angel Inn. Here were held from 1789, under the patronage of Lady Banks, wife of Sir Joseph of Revesby, erstwhile companion of Captain Cook on his first epic South Seas expedition, the Stuff Balls, held to encourage the local woollen cloth industry. Those attending this most exclusive occasion in the county year were supposed to wear clothes of Lincolnshire stuff. Meanwhile, downhill the leading townspeople mirrored their social superiors in the city assembly rooms, built over the Buttermarket in 1757. That had been built in 1736 out of the profits of ten years' civic banquets, donated by the Corporation. The new covered market for butter and poultry consisted of a double colonnade, with unglazed windows and with rows of forms for the 'good wives', who brought produce to market. A butchers' shambles was provided in 1774.

Horses were raced on Lincoln Heath south of the city in 1597, when the Corporation records note the Mayor's charges for a 'scaffold' (*ie*: a grandstand). In 1617 James I watched races over a quarter-mile course marked out with rails. After the Restoration in 1660 the Corporation sought to make racing a permanent fixture. In 1711 the Common Council subscribed to a plate. In 1716 the King gave a prize of a hundred guineas. Races on the flat and steeplechases were run over a four mile course on the Heath, commemorated in the name of the Three Horse Shoes public house at Waddington. After the Heath was enclosed the races moved to Welton and then to a new course marked out on the Carholme, where a new stand was built in 1806. Lincoln became the venue for the first meeting of the flat season. The Lincoln Handicap was first run on 10 August 1849, over a two mile course, later reduced to a mile-and-a-half, and then to the 'straight mile' in 1864.

The speed of the horse set the pace for contact between Lincoln and the outside world. In 1801 the old Lincoln waggons took six days to do the journey between London and Lincoln every week. In 1786, a new road was built up the eastern side, allowing wheeled traffic to avoid the steep gradient of the old High Street ascent between the upper and lower city. Before that, it could take a whole afternoon to drag a loaded waggon up the hill and the gentry had been accustomed to keep their carriages and horses uphill. Much is made of Lincoln's isolation before the railway but this did not stop a small stream of tourists, from Defoe (although he worked here) in the early eighteenth century to Washington Irving, surely one of the first American visitors, more than a century later.

One of these visitors, perhaps inevitably, was John Wesley, who preached in Lincoln for the first time on 30 June 1780, on Castle Hill at six in the evening, until a violent storm forced him and his congregation to shelter in the Court House, opened for them by the gaoler. Wesley returned twice, in 1787 and 1790, preaching on the latter occasion in the new house to 'hearers uncommonly serious' and walking in the Cathedral, which he preferred to York. Wesley thought Lincoln people had 'far more mildness and gentleness' than those of York. By then the Methodist Society in Lincoln had progressed from 'a kind of lumber room near Gowt's Bridge' to 'a neat and commodious chapel' holding about 600, on Waterside South between the High Bridge and the Brayford. As the Society expanded, so this chapel became too small and a larger building took its place in 1816, in turn replaced by a 'spacious and elegant' chapel for 1,500 worshippers in Clasketgate in 1837.

The Silver Street Free Methodist Chapel was built in 1865 on the site of the Zion Chapel belonging to the Countess of Huntingdon's Connexion. The oldest nonconformist churches in Lincoln dated from the years after the Commonwealth, when many people, unable to accept the restoration of the Church of England 'by law Established', were subjected to penal laws which made them 'dissenters'. Below the hill of Anglican establishment, dissent flourished. The Baptists had a place of worship on the site of the present church from the late seventeenth century, as did the Presbyterians, whose minister after the Restoration earned the approbation of the Anglican Bishop for his learning and worth. A fine Independent chapel in the Gothic style on Newland was rebuilt in 1876 to provide 1,100 sittings. The Friend's Meeting House in Beaumont Fee dates from 1685. A small Catholic chapel in the Bail was burned by the mob in 1688. A second chapel was then established near the Waterside and this, in turn, was moved to Bank Street in 1750. In 1799 a new chapel was built in Silver Street but in 1844 this was replaced by a church designed by Pugin.

While the idle rich made the round of race week, assemblies, the Stuff Ball, and the theatre, the idle poor moved in a different circle. They were regarded as a burden, parasites charged to the pockets of the better-off, on the rates collected by the overseers of the poor in each city parish. By 1740, however, under the provisions of Gilbert's Act, the thirteen city parishes had got together to set up a House of Industry, as a cheaper way to administer the provisions of the Elizabethan Poor Law in the face of a growing 'problem'. The intention was to keep the poor busy.

In 1799 the minute book refers to the repair of the Jersey wheels and an order to Claypole Mill in Nottinghamshire for hemp to be spun into sacking. This was 'women's work'. The men were hired out to break stones for road-mending, to brickmakers, or on farm work. In 1809 Joseph Lee was sent to work for Mr Doughty, ropemaker of Bailgate. Children were apprenticed to framework knitters in Nottinghamshire villages or sent into domestic service. One lad was apprenticed to a woman chimney sweep of St Peter-at-Gowts parish in 1810, presumably to work as a climbing boy. In 1797 the millowners of Bolton in Lancashire were paid five pounds to remove 22 pauper children, average age ten years. A few months later an anonymous complaint about their wellbeing came to the Directors of the House of Industry, but no action was taken. On the other hand, care was taken to provide the children in the House with education; a schoolroom was provided and lessons given by an inmate. Moreover, the diet was relatively generous by the standards of the time.

Unhappily this provision depended upon the poor being subjected to the discipline of an institution and its uniform. The men wore a blue coat with red collar (later modified to a grey suit), the women red flannel petticoat, dark cotton gown, black stockings and bonnet, and both displayed the copper badge of the House. On top of this, the poor were punished for offences against the rules: Catherine Smith was put on bread and water and confined for going outside without leave in 1799. This old workhouse was sold for £400 and removed in 1839. From 248 inmates in 1801, the numbers fell to 101 in 1831. In 1836 the Lincoln Union of 87 parishes, including the fifteen city ones, was formed under the Poor Law Amendment Act of 1834, and in 1837 a Union Workhouse for 360 was built on the hill near the asylum. Four years later it only held 173. Some help for the city's poor came from private bequests, funding annual doles. After 1653 such endowments had dried up and it was not until 1728 that Peter Richier MD left £12, from his estate at Ingoldmells and property in the Bail, for three poor widows below hill and two poor men of St Michael's parish.

Over the next 120 years, eleven charities were established, with a total investment of over £6,700. The income was issued in sums ranging from £2 18s to £4 10s per person, mainly in the parish of St Martin; possibly this area at the foot of the Strait had the highest level of poverty. By 1850 there were eighteen endowed charities dating from 1566 in Lincoln, against Gainsborough's twenty-seven. The Jersey School, established in Lincoln in the reign of Elizabeth, was endowed by Henry Stone of Skellingthorpe in 1693, to set poor children to work and teach them to spin, knit, and weave jersey. However, the improvements in machine spinning made such hand-spinning obsolete, and the Jersey School was abandoned in 1830, Henry Stone's bequest made over to Christ's Hospital School.

In 1744 a group of gentlemen and citizens met to consider a hospital for the city, although twenty-five years passed before their discussions bore fruit, with ten beds and accommodation for forty outpatients in a former maltings on Waterside South. In 1777 a purpose-built hospital with beds for twenty men and twenty women was established on the crest of the hill, south-east of the Castle so as to catch the sun. A few yards away to the west the so-called Lincoln Lunatic Asylum, otherwise known as The Lawn was set up in 1820, in an elegant building with a frontage 260 feet long, ornamented with a columned portico, in seven acres of grounds. The asylum was first mooted in 1803 by Paul Parnell, who provided £100 towards it, but The Lawn is most often associated with Dr E.P. Charlesworth who, with Mr Robert Gardiner Hill, practised the system called 'non-restraint', discarding the shackles and straitjackets 'with which the more refractory patients were sometimes tortured into confirmed madness; when kindness and vigilant attention to health, cleanliness, and comfort, would either have restored them to sanity or have made them happy and peaceful residents of the asylum'. Even the wall round the grounds was built below the edge of the hill, to allow an unrestricted view over the city, so that patients were not reminded of their confinement.

Further progress was made in 1784, when prison reformer John Howard visited the city gaol in the Stonebow. He found two separate rooms for male and female debtors upstairs and down below the dungeons for criminals, with earth floors, one containing a cage in which felons were locked at night. There was no water and no straw. Eighteen years later, Mr Nield described the gaol as one of the worst in the Kingdom, a disgrace to the city and shocking to humanity, where the prisoners were half-starved, half-suffocated, and in continual intoxication from the beer and spirits passed to them through the bars from people in the street. A new city prison and court house was completed in 1809, near the foot of the New Road leading up Lindum Hill, but in 1844 the prison was taken down and a new one for 40 prisoners built on the plan of the model prison at Pentonville, each prisoner having a separate cell with water tap, gas light and hammock. A police station was attached though the police office was then in Saltergate.

The Reform Act of 1832 removed the freemen's monopoly over the election of Lincoln's two MPs. Where formerly there had been over 1,200 freemen alone entitled to vote, Reform left only 514 living within the prescribed seven miles from the city and admitted 835 £10 householders to the franchise. The Municipal Corporations Act of 1835 did away with the old 45-man Corporation of 'The Mayor, Sheriffs, and Commonalty of the city of Lincoln' with its seven principal officers. Instead, a reformed Town Council of 25, with three principal officers, dispensed with the tradition of Corporation dinners at public expense, at which turtle soup had been a time-honoured dish. The Corporation dinner service and 300 dozen bottles of port and sherry were promptly sold off. A plan by the progressives to sell off the civic insignia as anachronistic was defeated, although ten years passed before the Mayor would again go in procession in blue gown and chain, preceded by sword and mace. However, the Mayor's chair and the Corporation seats 'which made the House of God a place for the fostering of pride and the exhibition of vanity' were taken out of St Peter-at-Arches Church and the custom whereby the Mayor and Corporation attended worship there in full dress was discontinued. Notwithstanding these reforms, feudalism survived in the Bail, which remained Duchy of Lancaster property, the courts leet, still summoned by the Duchy crier, continuing well into Victoria's reign. Furthermore, in the early part of the century the Dean and Chapter were opposed to all change, keeping the doors of the Cathedral locked, in token thereof.

Even here, however, the wind of change did blow. The reformers on the new Council wanted to replace the grammar school's Tudor curriculum of Greek and Latin with a more up-to-date programme. The Dean and Chapter, who appointed the master, resisted. In 1836 the Corporation exercised its right of control over the lower school and appointed an English master, whereupon pupil numbers increased; Tory families refused to allow their sons to enter the upper school, which dwindled to six boys. Eventually the Dean and Chapter agreed that the usher should, under the master, be responsible for such subjects as were necessary for a sound moral, religious, and liberal education.

The new arrangements coincided with the return of the recast Cathedral bells, including Great Tom, the third great bell in England, capable of holding 424 gallons and with room for a man to stand upright. Originally cast in a temporary foundry in Minster Yard in 1610, Great Tom had echoed over the Fens, from its place in the north-west tower — on Whit Sundays and when the judges came for the Assizes, until 1806 when, because its vibrations were endangering the tower, it ceased to be swung and the hours were struck with a hammer. In December 1827 Great Tom was found to be cracked and it remained silent until recast, together with two of the six Lady Bells, to make an even heavier Great Tom, in London in 1835. More than a decade before the railway came to Lincoln, this great bell, weighing almost five and a half tons, was transported by road from London and up the steep hill to the Cathedral, escorted by a vast procession. Great Tom had been given his voice back, to tell out times of change for Lincoln.

T: St Peter-in-Eastgate, destroyed in the Civil War. RIGHT: The Glory Hole from the west.

ABOVE: Lincoln was a garden city as shown in this picture by Joseph Baker. CENTRE: Signs of decay: the remains of St Swithun's and the Greyfriars. BELOW: John of Gaunt's Palace as it appeared in the eighteenth century.

ABOVE LEFT: This eighteenth century house in St Leonard's Lane incorporates materials from the demolished church. RIGHT: However, new churches downhill, such as St Martin's, reflected growing prosperity hand-in-hand with piety. CENTRE: The Corporation church, St Peter-at-Arches, c1720, 'a place for the fostering of pride and the exhibition of vanity'. BELOW LEFT: Houses on the east side of Minster Yard. New building began here in the late seventeenth century. RIGHT: The eighteenth century facade of the White Hart. Beyond is the former Angel Inn, headquarters of the Earl of Manchester in 1644.

ABOVE: The rear of the Harlequin, which housed Lincoln's first post-Restoration theatre. LEFT: Elegant classical buildings such as the County Hospital of 1777 designed by James Carr (now the Theological College) mark Lincoln's renaissance. INSET: The Lawn Hospital was established by Dr E. D. Charlesworth in 1820, to treat the mentally ill by non-restraint. RIGHT: Charlesworth's monument, in front of The Lawn, now the HQ of the Lincoln Archaeological Trust.

LEFT: These eighteenth century houses in Castle Square would be graceful even in Bath. RIGHT: The 'Number Houses' in Minster Yard, so-called because they were the first in Lincoln to be numbered, would do credit to Regency Brighton. BELOW: The new courthouse and city gaol which replaced the old prison condemned by John Howard.

ABOVE: The eighteenth century discovery of its classical heritage. The Southgate by Nathan Drake. BELOW: The romance of Roman ruins attracted enthusiastic amateur archaeologists. The Southgate by Nathan Drake.

ABOVE: An artist's impression of early nineteenth century Lincoln. The new county hospital between the castle and cathedral faces south to catch the sun. BELOW: The watercolours of Peter DeWint (1784–1849) depict Lincoln in the twilight of the Georgian era as a decaying rural backwater.

ABOVE: Later painters created an image of a Byzantine city held between soaring Cathedral and Brayford Pool, wharves crowded with the sails of many argosies. BELOW: Paintings like this by J.M.W. Turner appealed to the parvenue men of industry who were taking Lincoln over as the Victorian age came in.

94

Career of Prosperity

In February 1845 the *Lincolnshire Chronicle* reported that many shops in Lincoln were to be pulled down and rebuilt in the London style. The County Gaol and Hospital were to be enlarged and fifty new houses were to be built. In May the same newspaper observed that:

'Lincoln is pushing along her career of prosperity at a rate perfectly unexampled in her modern history. Jobbers Road will soon be occupied along the whole line right and left with handsome private houses. Mr. Hartley's new house near Cotton's Mill will soon be finished and the grounds are being laid out in a very tasty style. Mrs. Sympson is erecting a double house by the side of Mr. Hartley's, which will excel anything of the kind in Lincoln; the style is modern Italian.'

A year later the *Chronicle* reported that a row of handsome houses were nearing completion in Grantham Lane. New houses and places of business were being built and each one was let as soon as it was finished. In the summer of 1846 the demand for bricks in Lincoln had become so great that local brickyards were unable to cope and contracts were put out to Gainsborough. A year later bricks were still in short supply and there was a scarcity of houses. Two hundred were built in the four years alone from 1851 to 1855. In forty years from 1801 the number of houses in St Swithin's parish more than doubled. In St Mary's the number rose from 106 in 1801 to 562 by 1871 — a total that year in both parishes of 1,869. The population of Lincoln more than doubled 1801–1851, with the parishes of St Nicholas in Newport and St Swithin's showing the most growth.

How Victorian Lincoln developed is reflected in one street alone, Sincil Street, today still part of the busy shopping area around the covered market. In the mid-nineteenth century Sincil Street, located partly in St Swithin's and partly in St Mary-le-Wigford's, shared in the population growth. St Mary-le-Wigford increased from about 500 in 1801 to nearly 6,000 in 1901; St Swithin's rose from about 800 to 9,000. Yet before 1830 there was no Sincil Street. Hardly any houses or shops existed east of the ribbon development along High Street and below the Waterside. A 'common lane leading to St Mary' (St Mary-le-Wigford) was mentioned in 1719; known as Elder Lane in 1826, it probably followed the line of the present Sincil Street. A house and garden or orchard and a plot with a kilnhouse on it, east of this lane, with the Waterside to the north, had been removed by 1768, leaving just a paddock where Nixon's Court now stands. Although some sheds had been erected there by 1790, still no major building development had taken place in 1810.

In 1825, however, a plot of land with two newly erected dwelling houses was purchased by Robert Nixon. In five years six more houses had been put up on that plot. Nixon's original pair were numbered 1 and 2 Sincil Street, suggesting building had begun at the northern end. The order for renaming several Lincoln streets was made in 1830 and, when William White's *Directory* came out in 1842, Sincil Street existed. In 1866 property deeds still spoke of 'a street called Sincil Street which before its enlargement was called Elder Lane'. Enlargement was right. In 1842, less than twenty years after Nixon's initial purchase, Sincil Street comprised at least forty-six shops or houses, one referred to as Nixon's Court. In 1840 this was sold to George Gadsby, a grocer and hosier who already owned adjacent land. In 1859 he bought five more tenements known as Burley's Row, adjoining Nixon's Court, from William Clarkson who, in turn, had purchased them from William Burley. George Gadsby's will shows that by 1869 he owned 45–46 Sincil Street, his original property consisting of his own house and shop, five tenements in Nixon's Court (the former Burley's Row), and six other tenements.

So what became Sincil Street developed between 1825 and 1860, through the activity of local tradesmen, who bought up vacant sites along the old Elder Lane as a speculative development. This is reinforced by the records of a property not far from Nixon's Court. In 1869 George Squire, 'gentleman', sold his property in Sincil Street to grocer George Walker for £1,100. The land was bounded on the north by the common highway along the south side of the River Witham, on the south by the land and premises of George Baker, to the west by Sincil Street, and to the east by the premises of William Fotherby. It measured 56 by 63 feet. According to the deeds George Squire had built a dwellinghouse and shops comprising three messuages some time between 1855 and 1869.

The 1851 Census records the residents of the new street; 15–20 Sincil Street lay in St Mary's. They came from many parts; not one head of household originated in Lincoln. Of the twenty-nine occupants, ten came from outside Lincolnshire altogether, five from Scotland; only one was born in the city. The others came from villages within about twelve miles of Lincoln. Only three people were 50 or over; twenty-three were under forty. Here then in the low, plain, densely packed, new brick houses and shops lived a population of mostly young people, shop assistants, servants, apprentices, emigrants from the countryside, newcomers to city ways. Edmund Crossby kept a cow and sold milk.

What generated this development south of the Waterside and the influx of young people from the countryside? The answer lies partly in the Enclosure Act for Lincoln passed in 1803 and the Award completed in 1815. Without enclosure, the common rights over the open land around Lincoln would have still applied and the land could not have been built on. But it was the railway which really spurred development of Sincil Street. The Great Northern's station was sited near the southern end, which thus became a link between railway and Waterside. Naturally, shopkeepers and manufacturers wanted to establish themselves as close as possible to the new railway, its loading bays and its warehouses.

The growth of Lincoln meant the old street market was no longer adequate. In the year that George Hudson's first train reached Lincoln a noisy and, at times, bitter debate erupted over the choice of a new site. One issue was the likely effect of the railway link between Lincoln and the south Midlands and North of England on city trade. Hitherto there had been regular markets for corn in a small square enclosed with posts and chains on Cornhill, butter was sold in the High Street above the Stonebow and there was a general market along the High Street between St Mark's and the High Bridge. A butchery had been built in 1774, but the detritus from the slaughterhouse was discharged onto High Street. A fish market was held on the High Bridge. In addition to the weekly market, there were the annual fairs which also congregated along the High Street and in the streets adjoining, making them almost impassable and filthy. Already in 1810 one writer had observed that the street from the Cornhill to the Butter Market 'is, on a market day, literally choked up with stalls and standings to the great annoyance of passengers and inconvenience of the neighbouring housekeepers: it is indeed a nuisance which calls loudly for removal, and a grievance which it behoves the magistrates seriously and speedily to redress'. It was thirty years before that hope was fulfilled.

A public meeting on 14 April 1846 asked the Corporation to fix a permanent site for the city markets on or near the Cornhill. In case the Corporation decided against the expense, tradesmen and inhabitants formed a company, with a capital of £7,000 in 350 £20 shares, of which £3,200 had already been subscribed, and £3,000 more promised on the mortgage of a planned Corn Exchange and land to be bought on the east side of Cornhill. On 1 May 1846 a 'Memorial . . . to the Mayor, Aldermen and Burgesses of the City of Lincoln' announced the formation of the Company to build the Corn Exchange and make space for marketstalls near the Cornhill, and its intention to seek a lease for 75 years of a site on the Cornhill, and to buy the adjacent land.

An offer to write a clause into the lease allowing the Corporation to buy the Company out was opposed, because it might encourage the Corporation to purchase the site through an increase in the Borough rate. Here again Sincil Street epitomises a recurrent theme of Victorian Lincoln — the parsimony of the tribunes of the people. No reforms were to be undertaken that might require the Corporation to levy a borough rate and hence upset the electors. The Corporation's responsibilities must be restricted to those functions which could be covered by the Borough Fund alone, its income from rents, fees, tolls, and fines — for the quarter and petty sessions courts, the police, the gaol, the sewer taking away the refuse from the butchery, and the races, and nothing else.

In this case there was also anxiety that the Cornhill scheme might jeopardise a proposal to shift the sheep and cattle markets from St Swithin's Square to a new site. Farmers and graziers were reluctant to bring their animals into Lincoln over the cobbled streets and it was feared that, unless the market was improved, the railway companies would take stock to other markets. The cattle market was moved to a three acre site fitted up with pens 'having a commodious Inn at the entrance', on Monks Lane (Road) on Dean and Chapter land in 1849. Other opposition came from High Street shopkeepers, who feared the removal of the market from their doors would lead to a loss of trade and lower the value of their premises. However, as a letter writer explained, 'when it is considered how large a portion of the town that must now come between the Guildhall and the Toll-bar, when the new Railway Stations are taken into consideration and all the necessary increase of population and buildings which must necessarily surround them . . . if the Corporation will grant a lease of the Cornhill to the proposed Company for a Corn Exchange and Stall Market, so manifest and positive are the advantages of a market there, that the Shareholders need not fear the effect of competition in any other site likely to be offered to the public.'

The proposals were implemented and the foundation stone for the new Corn Exchange laid on the Cornhill in September 1847, on another of those gala days which Victorian Lincoln so enjoyed. The bells of St Peter's rang out their merriest peals as a procession from the Guildhall, led by the boys of Christ's Hospital, their band at its head, made its way to the Cornhill where, awaiting the civic party, were 'the beauty and fashion of Lincoln'. The new undertaking was under the control of the Lincoln Corn Exchange and Market Company, which had bought the site and the land adjoining for £7,000. The Exchange building and fixtures cost £12,000 and the Company borrowed £11,000, which it paid off by 1882. The remainder of the money was raised in £20 shares. The development of the Cornhill and the land adjoining further stimulated development along Elder Lane, leading to St Mary's Bridge. This now became a line of access between the new GNR station sited at St Mary's Bridge and the new market area on the land between the new Corn Exchange and the new Sincil Street. The Horse Fair remained on the High Street until 1929, when it was removed to the West Common. A new, larger Corn Exchange was opened in 1880.

Shops in Sincil Street supplied the requirements of stallholders and people attending the new market. Small traders and craftsmen were the typical pattern of the street's commercial life. Chatterton's appeared in 1892, beginning as bakers. Ashley's took over the glass and china business of Matthew Cockeril between 1892 and 1905. C.T. Parker's grocery and provision shop began during the same period. Sowerby's pork butchery began between 1877 and 1892. These are all still trading today but, from the beginning, there was a rapid turnover. In the fourteen years up to 1919 twenty-five businesses changed hands. Of those there in 1905 only two could trace their origins back thirty years. Moreover, in the 1880s, only four of the fifty-four premises in Sincil Street were occupied by their owners, most of the property being rented from landlords such as J. Spafford, who owned eight premises.

'Visitors to Lincoln will meet with every accommodation at the celebrated Cornhill Hotel Refreshment Rooms. Chops, steaks, soup, etc. on the shortest notice.' So ran an advertisement of a century ago. Then market clients could quench their thirst at two beerhouses and an inn and satisfy their hunger in two eating houses. The first fried fish shop appeared in 1905. A century ago traders included a cutler, an umbrella-maker, a brush-maker, and a photographer. Charles Warren's steam roundabouts spent the winter months behind the Black Goat Hotel and, until recently, some people in Lincoln could still remember his small fair tucked away in one of the yards off Sincil Street.

After the First World War, Sincil Street contained about forty-five traders and shopkeepers. At the Waterside end was George Metham, 'cycle fitter. Old farm workers in the villages round Lincoln could remember buying their first bikes there. Near Metham's was chimney sweep George Wilson, and further along was Sowerby's, the pork butchers. After Ashley's sewing machine agency and Goulson's, tobacconists, came Welsh, the music dealer and stationer. Then there was Mrs Barlow's confectionery, and another confectioner in Queen's Yard. Next to Hawksford and Kirby's the drapers was a jeweller's shop and next to this was Fletcher's butcher's shop. A musical instrument shop was next door to John Sharpe's confectioners. Next came Barlow's the newsagent, Ford's greengrocery, Mrs Little the milliner, and then Jonathan Varty Ltd, pork butcher and grocer.

There were many streets in Lincoln with a history not dissimilar from Sincil Street, whether it was the West End between Beaumont Fee and Carholme or the streets in St Peter-at-Gowts. It was the same story of old streets being widened or new streets being laid out. Broadgate was opened up in the 1840s to make a wider approach from the south for the increasing traffic coming into Lincoln. In the early sixties Lindum Terrace was developed as a row of fashionable villas. Guildhall Street was widened by the demolition of the City Arms Inn. In 1893 eight houses on the north-east side of the Cathedral were removed to create the present green (and Lord Tennyson's statue was erected). However, the plan, a year earlier, to take down and rebuild the Wren Library on another site was fortunately rejected.

These developments meant rising land values. One of the last areas to be so developed was the Monks Liberty, along Monks Road where nine inhabited houses occupied by 43 people in 1891 ten years later became 269 houses with 1,217 inhabitants. However, the streets in these down-hill parishes were low-lying and damp, the houses densely-packed, and conditions appalling, even by Victorian standards. As late as 1886 the infant mortality rate for Lincoln was three times the national average. Small wonder then that a Burial Board was established in 1854 and that a cemetery had been opened in 1856 on 15 acres of the Cow Paddle on the South Common. Forty years later there were two more cemeteries, on Washingborough Road and Newport.

For those unable to afford a private doctor or a club, the Lincoln Dispensary was established on the Cornhill in 1826. In 1855 it treated 1,753 patients; in 1895 it was treating 1,535 at home and 1,468 out-patients, as well as 457 casualties. In 1907 it moved to Silver Street, treating 1,450 home and 1,394 out-patients and in 1928 1,278 home and 1,254 out. The Dispensary moved to Mint Street in 1936 where, after 1948, it became the NHS Chest Clinic. In spite of enlargements to the County Hospital in 1845 and '54, by 1877 poor sanitation, an inadequate water supply and insufficient fresh air instigated another move, to a new site east of Lindum Terrace; the new hospital was opened by Lord Brownlow in 1878. By 1907 it provided 120 beds and had a special children's ward, a newly equipped operating theatre, and the latest electrical and sterilising appliances. A new ward and nurses' home were added in 1914 and in 1922 an X-ray department and laboratory installed as a war memorial. Further enlargements were made between 1930 and 1936.

In 1864 Mrs Anne Fector Bromhead had started a fund to supply additional nurses for the County Hospital and her Institute of Nurses was founded in 1867, to supply nursing in patients' homes 'and for gratuitous attention to the poor of the city'. By 1885 they were working in every city parish. In 1876 The Red House was established in Nettleham Road (the private hospital known, since 1923, as The Bromhead) and ten years later, in memory of Mrs Bromhead, it was decided to provide a sanatorium for nurses working among infectious diseases. In 1907 further buildings were added to commemorate Miss Henrietta Bromhead. In 1847, 25 acres of the Red Hall Estate was bought for £30,000 for the County Lunatic Asylum.

In May 1845 the *Chronicle* reported plans for a Water Company, established in 1846. A waterworks was completed in 1850 at a cost of £24,000, when water was to be conveyed into houses 'forthwith'. A steam engine raised water from the Prial Brook in Skellingthorpe and from the upper Witham into a 23-acre reservoir in Skellingthorpe and thence, *via* the filter beds at Boultham, could supply it to any room of a house. However, in the 1850s and '60s the Witham and Fossdyke were so choked with filth as to constitute a considerable health hazard. The ancient St Mary's conduit was rebuilt in 1864. Some manufacturers, such as the brewers, emptied the conduits early in the morning by fetching water in tubs borne on poles by two porters, leaving poor people without water for their early morning tea. The city's main water supply came from the reservoir at Hartsholme but Lincoln's tap water was polluted with sewage, which seeped into the Witham from the middens of the expanding suburbs of Bracebridge and Boultham. Moreover, Grantham and other towns above Lincoln discharged their effluent into the Witham too. Nevertheless the City Council, supported by a public meeting, refused to adopt the Infectious Diseases (Notification) Act and in 1895 the Medical Officer of Health reported that few towns had a better health record or lower death rate than Lincoln. Such hubris brought its own retribution. In December 1904 typhoid broke out.

Within a month the disease had claimed eighteen victims. 13,000 handbills were distributed, requiring all drinking water and milk to be boiled. Emergency accommodation for typhoid cases was rapidly arranged at Long Leys Hospital and various local halls, and a staff of officials and nurses were organised. By 24 February 1905 there were 697 cases and 49 deaths. Long queues formed to collect the daily supplies of pure water from the Midland Railway yard. Huge bottles of water were brought in from Potter Hanworth and Market Rasen and the GNR supplied 30,000 gallons a day from the artesian wells at Willoughby, transported in twelve tenders. Twenty-three collection points were established. Newark Urban District Council offered 200,000 gallons per day but their price was considered too high. This did not stop people from travelling to Newark to collect it. A Ladies' Committee was formed and sheets, blankets, shirts, nightgowns, dressing gowns and flannel and cotton jackets were made and distributed from their depôt at Atherstone Place. By April 1905, 900 cases had been notified and there were outbreaks in neighbouring villages. The Great Northern station master died, as did the president of the Lincoln Co-op, a prominent local preacher. Convalescents were sent to the coast or to Drinsey Nook on the Fossdyke. After six months the epidemic died out. There had been 1,023 cases and 127 deaths. The end was marked by a service of thanksgiving in the Cathedral.

ABOVE: Compare this painting of the Brayford with the next. CENTRE: This painting shows how busy Lincoln had become by Peter DeWint's time. BELOW: The Sincil Dyke, by Peter DeWint.

ABOVE: The Sincil Dyke by Peter DeWint. Soon after these pictures were
made, this area disappeared under streets of terraced houses. BELOW: The
High Street looking north, by A.C. Pugin, c1800. The Stonebow, the tower
of St Peter-at-Arches, and the High Bridge obelisk are obvious landmarks.

ABOVE LEFT: The High Bridge obelisk erected in 1763. RIGHT: New shop fronts replaced the old stall-fronted shops. CENTRE: The new magistrates' courts in the Castle grounds. BELOW: The High Street in Dickens's time. The road surface is cobbled and street lamps and pavements have appeared.

ABOVE: Replacing the cobbles on Castle Square with flagstones, by an unknown artist. BELOW: Repairing Cobb Hall (or preparing the gallows?) by DeWint's contemporary, Frederick Mackenzie.

ABOVE: The graveyard for hanged felons within the Lucy Tower. BELOW: The prison chapel, designed so no prisoner could see another or sit comfortably. OPPOSITE ABOVE: The Exchequer Gate enclosed a deeply conservative religious establishment. CENTRE: However, the Newland Independent church of 1840 in 'lancet Gothic style' bespeaks a flourishing anti-establishment religious current. RIGHT: The Diocesan Training College of 1842, now Bishop Grosseteste College of Higher Education. BELOW: St Nicholas (1838), Sir Giles Gilbert Scott's earliest church.

ABOVE: The market held within the Duchy of Lancaster's purview in Castle Square — W.G. Herdman. BELOW: The market stalls along the High Street, 1841.

Wheels of Industry

In June 1846 a crowd watched as the first locomotive, drawing a carriage-load of people, steamed into Lincoln over the Midland Company's tracks. In August the official opening of the line from Nottingham was a gala occasion. Shops were closed, the minster bells rung, and flags were flying when the special train carrying the 'Railway King' himself, George Hudson, rolled into Lincoln. Every viewpoint was packed with spectators and the band of the 4th Irish Dragoon Guards played the *Railway Waltz* as the train departed from Lincoln at 12 noon on its return run.

By contrast the opening of the Great Northern line two years later was performed without ceremony, except that the Lincoln-Hull mailcoach drove into the city in mourning sable, the horses in funeral plumes, and the press prophesied that soon there would be no more stage coaches. Even so, when it came to an affair of the heart, the traditional forms of transport had perhaps more romance. So it was when Miss Betsy Rudgard, second daughter of Alderman Rudgard, eloped with a Mr Wig of Liverpool in September 1848. The 'sighing Romeo', having taken a fly from the Saracen's Head, his Juliet 'stepped in at the Canwick bar'. However, at the Halfway House (at Swinderby) the driver refused to go any further and 'the lovers betook themselves in a market cart to Newark and the railway'. The lady's brother followed in hot pursuit by train but got to Liverpool just in time to congratulate the newly-weds.

Barely five years after the first train, the two railway companies were vying with each other to carry passengers to the Great Exhibition of 1851. Three years later it was Lincoln's turn, when the Royal Agricultural Show was held on the Cowpaddle. Now the nation's manufacturers of agricultural implements beat a path to Lincoln and 'the railway officials were at their wit's end to get the mechanical wonders arriving by every train safely delivered'. The railway companies conveyed agricultural machinery to Lincoln and back at a single tariff; stock was transported free. This was a considerable undertaking, given that the railways were only eight years old. The show area was 1,000 feet long by 600 feet wide. Implement trials were held at Greetwell Farm and on a trial yard near the Showground. For the duration of the Royal Show the High Street was a forest of flags and evergreen-decked triumphal arches and the Guildhall was hung with variegated lamps surrounded by a crown. Open-air concerts were held in the Temple Gardens and Wombwell's Menagerie provided further entertainment.

Early in the spring of 1847, one of the vessels belonging to Mr E.W.R. Rudgard, common brewer and maltster of Waterside North, loaded with 240 quarters of wheat and 12 quarters of peas, went down in the Castleford Canal, Leeds. That reminds us that Lincoln's oldest industrial base was the processing of agricultural produce, and that depended on the waterway network with the heavy industry of South Yorkshire and the West Riding. Ten years before the railway came, the Lincoln end of this network was so unsatisfactory it was said it took as long to get from Hull to Lincoln as it took to cross the Atlantic. The channel was too shallow, craft frequently went aground on shoals, and the bridge at Torksey was too low. In 1846 Richard Ellison, whose family had operated the navigation on lease from Lincoln Corporation since the eighteenth century, granted a sublease to the Great Northern Railway. Not surprisingly the railway company was not prepared to operate the waterway as a going concern in competition with its own trains. It allowed the channel to deteriorate to such an extent that four men and two horses took four hours to haul a 40-ton load of coal the mile from the Pyewipe Inn to the Brayford. At the same time the railway company ran cheap trains to Boston, forcing the Witham steam packets off the river.

The late forties were lean years. In May 1847 distress was reported among mechanics and small traders. Foundry and building workers planned a meeting to persuade employers to increase wages. A week later bricklayers and stonemasons came out on strike. These circumstances may have helped make Lincoln's working people unduly susceptible to the blandishments of a party of charlatans who, in the early autumn of 1847, offered them a chance to exchange their situation as wage-earners for that of independent smallholders. In July 1847 the Red Hall estate at Bracebridge Heath on the southern outskirts of Lincoln was bought by Thomas Allsop of Exchange Buildings in the City of London. What no-one knew at the time was that the 373-acre estate had been bought on behalf of the Chartist leader, Feargus O'Connor. However, by September, the newspapers were reporting rumours which claimed that O'Connor intended to divide the Red Hall Estate into cottage lots of four acres and to set up a Chartist Colony. Meetings were held at the Green Dragon Inn to explain the scheme and a branch of the National Land Company was formed with eleven members. *The Lincolnshire Chronicle* proclaimed in November 'O'Connor and the Chartists are endeavouring to prevail upon the hard working men of Lincoln to join their land swindle . . .'. *The Stamford Mercury*, on the other hand, was optimistic, seeing a ready market for the produce which each smallholding would grow.

The story now took a farcical turn. The President of the Lincoln branch of the National Land Company was Charles Stewart, a 30-year-old plasterer, who had been living in Lincoln for two years and was bigamously married to the sister of Mr Harrison, butcher of Dunholme. In the spring of 1848, he was in Lincoln Gaol for stealing a pair of garters and so was unable to preside at a Chartist meeting at the Green Dragon addressed by the sinister, inebriated, and incoherent Dr Peter Murray McDouall, advocate of violent action, who called upon the men of Lincoln to fight for their rights. The *Chronicle* reported that the crowd had begun larking about and one man had been 'burked' with a bucket of whitewash. In April 1848 the Chartists held their mass demonstration on Kennington Common and in May, Feargus O'Connor came to Lincoln to conduct the auction of allotments. Thirteen cottages had been built on the Red Hall Estate, each standing in four acres. The Red Hall itself and 60 acres were, so it was rumoured, to be set aside for an agricultural college. Here, it was announced, was a most favourable investment for the small capitalist or tradesman. In fact the sale resulted in the disposal of five lots only instead of the anticipated 91. Far from realising the expected £550–£750 only £50 an acre was raised. In all only fifteen acres were sold. Lot 6 went to W.H. Brooke, brewer and maltster of the Waterside, Lincoln; Lot 2 went to that Lincoln brewer and maltster, E.W.R. Rudgard, whose vessel had sunk in the Castleford Canal; Lot 3 went to Joseph Pepperdine, a Lincoln timber merchant and dealer in building supplies.

In the evening O'Connor spoke for an hour and a half in the newly-built Corn Exchange to a capacity audience, recalling the time when it would have been a bold man who preached the doctrines of democracy in a cathedral city. If those who were paid to instruct the people in the holy principles of the Bible had done their duty, it would not have been left to a stranger to come and instruct the labour class in their rights.

Had O'Connor but known it, things were changing in Lincoln. New industries were springing up. In the previous April the *Chronicle* had observed that the new trade of iron-founding had developed in Lincoln within the past few years and now gave work to upwards of 200. In 1842 Clayton, a former Witham steamboat skipper, and his partner Shuttleworth, had begun making steam engines and later threshing machines, and in 1845 produced the first portable engine. Their Stamp End works extended over eight acres and, by 1864, employed about 1,400 men. As employers they were notable for providing a dining room (not 'canteen') for their workforce. In 1845 Charles Duckering began making stoves, mantelpieces and sanitary ironwork, as well as corn mills and agricultural machinery. Six years later former miller William Foster began producing threshing machines and other farm machinery. In 1854 Robert Robey established himself in a wooden workshop on Canwick Road, making iron-framed threshing engines and in the same year exhibited a portable engine at the Royal Show in Lincoln on land later to be occupied by Robey's works. In 1857 Joseph Ruston joined Burton and Proctor's millwright's business at the Sheaf ironworks on Waterside, which henceforth became known as Ruston, Proctor, & Co. From 25 employees, the firm grew until, by 1889, it gave employment to over 1,600.

Until now Lincoln could have been regarded as a somewhat decayed cathedral city and market town. It would have been difficult to portray it as a thriving city of the industrial north. Yet, in the mid-nineteenth century, tall factory chimneys and high mill walls were more typical of Lincoln than the lofty pinnacles of the Cathedral. In December 1855 the man most strikingly symbolic of the old order died. Colonel Charles de Laet Waldo Sibthorp of Canwick, MP for Lincoln, had opposed Catholic Emancipation, the Reform Bill, Municipal Reform, the New Poor Law, and the Great Exhibition of 1851. He had an implacable detestation of railways. Charles Dickens described him as 'this ferocious-looking gentleman, with a complexion almost as sallow as his linen', and huge black moustache. 'Can anything be more exquisitely absurd than the burlesque grandeur of his air, as he strides up to the lobby, his eyes rolling like those of a Turk's head in a cheap Dutch clock?' His death marked a watershed. Henceforward the rich, Liberal, new industrialists — men like Clayton, Shuttleworth, and Ruston — dominated political life. Their hands were felt on every part of the life of the city downhill, as patrons of change, whereas it often seemed that the Church and 'uphill' stood for all that was reactionary. Schools, hospitals, charities, parks and gardens, which in the Age of Faith had been the province of the Church, now were presented to the city out of the benevolence of the factory owners. Ruston's private collection of paintings would one day form the nucleus of the Usher Gallery, available for every citizen to admire.

Hitherto the good citizens of Lincoln, provided they could afford the family subscription of twenty shillings a year, or five shillings for a single ticket, could avail themselves of the pleasures of the Temple Gardens on the hillside below the ruins of the Bishop's Palace, to hear the band or walk among the 'Roman, Norman, Saxon, [sic] and other antiquities', and enjoy the view from one of the numerous seats and arbours. Or there was The Promenade, created in 1844 along the edge of the hill overlooking the South Common, from which a striking panorama of the city could be obtained.

In August 1872, however, the streets were once again crowded with excited people, the occasion the official opening of the Arboretum — twelve acres of ornamental grounds, beautifully laid out over the old Monks Leys, one of the commons of the city since the Reformation. The celebrations marked the conclusion of a project in progress since September 1869. By May 1872 the terrace wall, the fountain basins and the stone steps up the terrace were ready and the contracts for the pavilion, the lodge, and the principal entrance gates in hand. The Arboretum, it was said (with an amazing display of adjectives), had now assumed a neat and finished appearance, and in the course of a few years, when the numerous trees and evergreens planted in it had made some growth so as to develop their several marked peculiarities and individual attractions and beauty, would, with its 'deciduous conifer evergreens [sic]' become one of the greatest attractions of the city.

Early in August the monster stone lion was conveyed from the railway station to the Arboretum on a trolley lent by Messrs Clayton and Shuttleworth and drawn by a traction engine lent by Messrs Robey and Co, reaching the gate of the Arboretum by 9 pm, where it was left until the morning. So heavy was it that overnight the wheels of the trolley sunk a foot into the ground. Now the great day had come. The bands of the Royal Engineers, the Robin Hood Rifles, the Leeds Model Band, the Lincoln Militia and the Lincoln Rifle Corps, to say nothing of the handbell ringers known as the Lincoln Campanologium, provided the music, while a procession including such diverse attractions as Miss Lizzie Gilbert's troupe of performing Lilipudlian Ladies, Professor Banzo's performing dogs and all the trades of Lincoln passed through the banner-hung streets, under the decorative arch at the entrance to Monks Road, having first partaken of a *déjeuner* at the Mayor's expense in the Corn Exchange. Once arrived at the Arboretum, Mr Joseph Wells of the Crystal Palace, gave a fireworks display (presumably in broad daylight), there was a balloon ascent, and a 'quantity of music to which the people danced right merrily'.

At the Mayor's arrival at the Arboretum a number of young girls dressed as fairies appeared, bearing scrolls supposed to have been written by the Monks who had once held the Leys, and these proceeded to render up possession to the Mayor. *Benedicite* was then sung, followed by Psalm 148 *Laudate Dominum*, and the Bishop offered a prayer with the inauspicious invocation: 'Oh Almighty God, maker of all things, who at the beginning didst plant a garden in Eden and didst put man therein . . .'. The other name for the Arboretum was 'the People's Park' and it was intended to

'encourage home associations by drawing the men, the breadwinners of the family, away from those temptations and means of debasement which seemed inseparable from life in large towns and cities, . . . by tempting a man to enjoy himself with his wife and family in preference to accepting the pleasure of the public house. . . .'.

Lincoln's engineering firms built a reputation with a number of 'firsts'. In 1875 Robey's produced a winding engine, the first of many, for the Duke of Sutherland's pits. A Robey engine powered the first electric lighting in the City of London. Robey's workshops were the first in England to be lit by electricity, using the first Edison dynamo imported. At the Paris International Exhibition in 1878 Robey's took a gold medal with the only engine not to break down during the entire Exhibition. Twenty years later they built the gold mining stamp batteries for Johannesburg and, in 1902, the world's first long-distance wireless station at Poldhu was equipped with Robey steam engines and boilers. Not to be outdone, Joseph Ruston received the Legion d'Honneur and in 1900 Ruston and Proctor took the highest number of awards of all British competitors at the Paris Universal Exhibition. By 1907 Clayton and Shuttleworth had 1,500 employees scattered through Eastern Europe in their branches in Vienna, Prague, Budapest, Breslau, Krakow, Odessa, and Bucharest.

Meanwhile the Victorian technological dream was bringing new amenities to the city itself. Already in 1842 the streets were lit for nine months of the year by new street lamps. The new pipes heated by steam must have been welcomed by the congregation of St Martin's Church when they were installed in January 1845. At the same time the pulpit of St Peter-at-Arches was fitted with two naptha lamps. A month later it was proposed to light St Martin's by camphine lamps, the Church having been lit by 'a few common dips'. The first Gas Works was established in 1828 near the Brayford, providing a supply for seventy-six street lamps and a few private consumers. In 1855 a New Gas Light and Coke Company was set up in competition and in 1885 this was taken over by the city. The original works in Carholme Road were turned into a distribution centre and the works at Bracebridge, constructed in 1876, were rebuilt in 1932.

The hive of industry is the emblem of the Lincoln Equitable Industrial Co-operative Society. Lincoln Co-op was formed in 1861 in premises in Silver Street. By 1896 it had seventeen branch stores which, by 1922, had increased to twenty-eight and to thirty-two by 1937. Besides its trading object, the Co-op also sought the 'domestic, social and intellectual advancement of its members' (numbering nearly 25,000 in 1930) and provided a library and newsroom, free of charge.

Education began to be seen not so much as a means of keeping the lower orders in the place in which it had pleased God to set them, but as an agent for change in society. There was considerable interest in providing schools for the working classes, in spite of the lady who told Chancellor Benson that she and her sister preferred 'an ignorant poor'. By the 19th century the Blue Coat School occupied a large red brick building on St Michael's Mount. Other benefactors augmented the foundation; by 1856, 124 boys were taught music, as well as reading, writing, and arithmetic. The Lincoln Central National Schools in Silver Street were established in 1813. An infants' school was started in Langworthgate in 1829 and another was established out of public subscription in 1831 at the north-west corner of the Grey Friars. The foundation stone of the Victoria Infants' School in St Peter-at-Gowts parish was laid on the day of the Queen's coronation in 1838. Wesleyan Day Schools in Grantham Street were begun in 1840, followed in 1841 by the British School in Newland and the Diocesan Training School in Newport.

By 1858 there were sixty-five public schools catering for over 5,000 children and forty-two private schools accommodating 1,065 children. In 1859 the Wesleyan Schools for infants, boys, and girls, in Rosemary Lane were built. Said at that time to be 'the largest educational establishment in Lincolnshire', they provided accommodation for 600 children but had 638 on the books and an average weekly attendance of 500 in 1864. They were notable for the covered play area and drawing room for the boys, the dining rooms, hot water central heating, gas lighting, and 70-foot tower surmounting the main entrance. The view from the master's house covered the entire playground.

Begun in a garret in the Corn Exchange in 1863, before moving in 1864 to the upper floor of the Corporation Offices in Silver Street, a 'School of Science and Art' was established on land on the north side of Monks Road twenty years later. It cost £8,000, raised by voluntary contributions, and a grant from the Department of Science and Art. Six years later the Corporation provided additional workshops. A larger chemistry laboratory was added in 1896 and, in 1901, the school was taken over by the Corporation, in its new capacity as the local education authority, as the City School. There were three departments — the School of Art, the Technical Day School, and the Evening School for Science, Engineering, and Commercial Subjects — catering for more than 800 students. In 1907 the buildings were further expanded.

In 1875 Chancellor Benson, the future Archbishop of Canterbury, began night classes for working men, taught by students of the recently established theological college. Over 400 men turned up on the opening night in the Central School in Silver Street. St Andrew's Church of England School was opened in 1883. A 'babies' room' was added five years later. Bishop King Elementary School was opened in 1900. The first school built by the City Council under the 1902 Education Act was Monks Road School for infants and juniors, opened in 1905. In 1920 senior departments were formed and in 1935 the senior pupils were moved to the Rosemary Road and Spring Hill schools. The Spring Hill School for Infants, opened in 1910, became a girls' secondary school in 1929. In 1930 Skellingthorpe Road Junior School opened its doors. The marriage registers of the city's Anglican parishes suggest that illiteracy had all but been eliminated by 1900.

On the east end of the Grey Friars building a small brick extension represents the first adult education building in Lincoln. The Corporation in 1833, granted the use of the crypt of the Grey Friars to the Mechanics Institute, for a library and museum, and the upper room for lectures and exhibitions. Before 1673 the Rector of Waddington had donated to his birthplace 'a Fair Library for the use of the Masters and Ministers of the Town' adjoining the Free School. The Lincoln Joint Stock Library was set up in 1814 and, from 1843, occupied premises in Mint Lane. In 1856 it had 278 subscribers and housed 13,000 books. The New Permanent Library was formed in 1822 and was incorporated in the Mechanics Institute, holding 5,000 books for 380 members, including 70 juveniles. However, the reformed grammar school took over the entire Grey Friars building, so the Mechanics Institute moved to a new site in Broadgate and subsequently to the Guild Court on Danes Terrace. By 1895 its library housed 20,000 volumes.

A few years later the Mechanics Institute had merged with the Church House and Institute, established first in Westgate but moved in 1889 to the old Christ's Hospital buildings. The Institute included a gymnasium, recreation rooms, carpentry workshop, classrooms and library, and activities included cricket, football, shooting, and cheap summer holidays in Britain and on the Continent. At the County News Room on Castle Hill and the City News Room at the Corn Exchange it was possible to read the newspapers. The YMCA in Guildhall Street also had a library of about 1,000 books and the Lincoln Club in St Mary's Street included a large reading room.

The City of Lincoln Public Library was established under the Public Libraries Act in the old Assembly Rooms over the Butter Market in Silver Street in 1894. In 1895 it had 7,000 books and news and reading rooms were opened in that year. In 1913 the library was transferred to a new building designed by Sir Reginald Blomfield in Free School Lane and built with a Carnegie grant. By 1922 the library had 16,000 books, increasing to 38,000 in 1930, and 48,000 in 1937. A branch library was opened at Bracebridge in 1927. In this year the Usher Gallery, endowed from the bequest of James Ward Usher, was opened.

Nor were citizens' spiritual needs neglected. The one and only Census of Religious Worship in 1851 showed attendances at the city's free churches on·Sunday mornings over the previous year averaged almost twice those of the Anglican churches (although attendance at Anglican evening services was slightly higher). St Peter-at-Eastgate and St Peter-at-Arches had the largest Anglian congregations, followed by the Cathedral. However, the Wesleyans had by far the biggest congregations. As the city limits expanded, new churches and chapels followed. The Free Churches led the way, building nine new chapels between 1863 and 1885, including the Wesleyan church in Bailgate and the Thomas Cooper Memorial Church in St Bene't's Square, at over £32,000.

The Anglican impetus came somewhat later. Under Bishops Wordsworth and King, between 1870 and 1904, at least £54,000 was spent to build seven new churches and restore or enlarge six others, using the best-known architects of the ecclesiological movement. In 1867 the foundation stone of St Swithin's Church was laid; the new St Peter-in-Eastgate was opened in 1870 followed, in 1871, by the new St Mark's Church. St Andrew's was erected in 1876, using material from the old church of St Martin, and was formed into a parish in 1883. St Paul-in-the-Bail, designed by Sir A.B. Blomfield (who had also designed St Peter's), was completed in 1877. St Faith's in Charles Street was built in 1885, to C. Hodgson Fowler's design, as a mission church attached to St Mary-le-Wigford, becoming the parish church of the expanding West End of the city in 1899. Fowler also designed All Saints, Monks Road, the gift of the industrialist, Alfred Shuttleworth, consecrated in 1904 for the newly built-up Monks Road.

The Catholic church of St John, built by Pugin in Silver Street in 1854, was pulled down and a new church dedicated to St Hugh built on Monks Road in 1893, at a cost of £8,000. (A chapel of ease attached to St Hugh's was set up on the St Giles estate in 1933.) Nationwide, religious observance was said to be in decline, yet more than £94,000 was spent on building or enlarging twenty places of worship in just over forty years — reminiscent of the spate of church-building in Lincoln in the eleventh and twelfth centuries.

The Anglican church-builders were getting less for their money by the end of the nineteenth century than their Nonconformist counterparts had thirty years before. The average cost of a nonconformist chapel in the years 1863–80 was £2,800, compared to £6,626 for an Anglican church in 1877–1904. Nor was this necessarily a case of nonconformist architecture being more simple and austere. The Anglican church of St Nicholas, built in 1840, cost £2,500 whereas St Andrew's, nearly forty years later, cost £6,000. The parish of St Giles, serving the new council house estate on the north-east of the city, was created in 1932 and the church, largely a rebuilding of St Peter-at-Arches, which had been pulled down in 1932 to relieve traffic congestion, was consecrated in 1936. At the same time St Bene't's, closed for seventy years, was restored and reopened.

Meanwhile the fabric of the Cathedral was giving cause for concern. Restoration work in the 1870s had barely been completed when the whole of the parapet on one side of the central tower was swept away in a storm and complete reconstruction was necessary. In 1921 all three towers were in danger of collapse. For the first time ever, the technique of drilling by compressed air and grouting under air pressure was used on an historic building. In addition, bronze cramps and reinforced concrete beams were employed. The bells were lowered 30 feet and housed in a new bellchamber so that, although their sound can still be heard eight miles away, the sound in the immediate neighbourhood is negligible. The cost of all this was £135,000, of which £20,000 was given by the Pilgrim Trust and £35,000 by Americans in memory of their Lincolnshire forebears, a fresh example of the New World being called to help the Old, and the first of many examples of transatlantic generosity towards the Cathedral.

As the population of the city increased so its limits expanded. In 1882 a private company began to operate horse-drawn trams from Bracebridge along the High Street into the city. This utility was acquired by the Corporation in 1905 for £10,489 and electric trams were substituted, the tram sheds located at Bracebridge. Lincoln's was the first tramway system to install a surface contact system, which operated by means of electrified iron studs placed at short intervals between the running rails. Current collection was by a shoe in contact with the studs. A battery-operated magnet in the tram lifted the studs from below road level to contact with the collecting shoe. Defects developed after fourteen years and an overhead wire system was used until 1929, when motor 'buses took over. By 1912 New Boultham existed and in 1920 Bracebridge had been incorporated into the city, whose population rose from 61,346 in 1911 to 66,020 in 1921, slowing to 66,243 in 1931.

The High Street in 1848, by John Ferneley, two years after the coming of the railway.

ABOVE: The High Street prior to the coming of the railway. BELOW:
Nineteenth century factory chimneys challenge the primacy of the cathedral
for Lincoln's skyline.

LEFT: The railway tried but never quite finished the trade on the Witham.
RIGHT: The old works along Waterside South from Thornbridge.
BELOW: The cattle market also moved to Monks Road in 1849.

115

ABOVE: One of the O'Connor plots on Brant Road. CENTRE: This building on the Witham recalls the prestige of the Lincoln Cooperative Society. BELOW: Some of the last Victorian terraces were built off Monks Road in a grid of twenty-four streets.

ABOVE LEFT: The Arboretum was laid out over the old Monks Leys in 1872. RIGHT: The Lion was the gift of Alderman Clarke, a local chemist, who patented a popular brand of pills for the blood. BELOW LEFT: The gay cast-iron bandstand of 1884. RIGHT: It was hoped the Arboretum would divert men from public houses, to spend time with their families.

LEFT: Tennyson's Statue. RIGHT: The City Library, 1906, by Sir
Reginald Blomfield, who also designed the Usher Gallery, 1927. BELOW:
The Constitutional Club and Broadgate suggest late Victorian confidence.

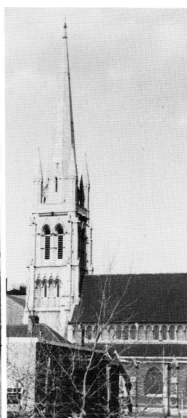

LEFT: The 780-foot Palladian south front of the County Pauper Lunatic Asylum, Bracebridge, of 1849, now St John's Hospital. RIGHT: St Swithun's, 1869–87, by James Fowler. BELOW: The County Hospital, 1878, by Alexander Graham.

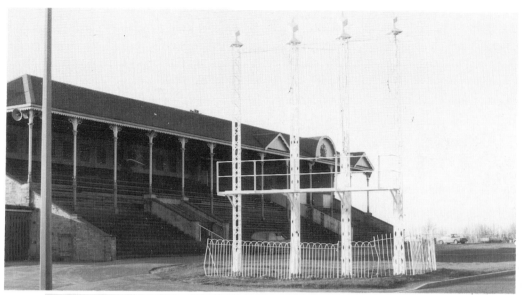

ABOVE: The Grandstand, 1826; iron verandah with Doric columns.
BELOW: The North District National School, Westgate, now the Castle
Hotel.

120

LEFT: The City School, 1885–6, Dutch Renaissance; founded for the study of arts and sciences. RIGHT: The Theological College alias the Scholae Cancellarii or Bishop's Hostel, founded by Bishop Wordsworth and Chancellor Benson 1874. BELOW: The Old Barracks, now the Lincolnshire Life Museum: Lincoln became a regimental headquarters again in the nineteenth century.

ABOVE: The Stonebow in 1906. Statute hirings were still held here.
BELOW: These views of the High Street show how relatively deserted the
streets were at the turn of the century.

Fit for Heroes

Less than a decade after the typhoid epidemic, the war to end all wars began. 971 Lincoln men and one woman lost their lives. The prizewinning expertise of Lincoln companies, household names in the cities of the Central Powers, were now diverted to armaments manufacture. During the latter part of the war Lincoln became a leading aircraft construction centre.

Ruston, Proctor and Co received their first order from the War Office in January 1915. A special factory was built on waste ground beside the Witham at Boultham and test flights took place from hangars beside Alderman's Walk on the West Common. Ruston Proctor and Ruston and Hornsby built 2,750 'planes, as well as engines and Lewis guns, giving work to 3,000 men and women. They were the first firm to build the Sopwith *Camel* and it was a Ruston-built plane that brought down the Zeppelin 8L11 in September 1916, its pilot winning a VC. From May 1915 until two months before the Armistice, Robey's built about 300 aircraft, including the Robey seaplane, Sopwith 806 *Gunbus* (was this the forerunner of the modern 'gunship'?), and the Peters' *Fighting Machine*, named after J.A. Peters, Robey's design chief. Robey's had an aerodrome at Bracebridge Heath and aircraft shops in Coultham Street. Clayton and Shuttleworth also went over to building aircraft and one of their Sopwith *Camels* helped to shoot down the German air ace, von Richthofen. However, it was, with a terrible irony, their experience in producing agricultural machinery, developed and demonstrated by Lincoln's manufacturers in numerous international exhibitions and at the Royal Agricultural Show in Lincoln eight years before, which attracted the attention of the War Office. As early as 1870 Robey's of Lincoln had built the first road steamers on rubber tyres for the War Office. In 1907, the year after the Royal Show, Hornsby's managing director, David Roberts, had begun experiments on a caterpillar tractor. The prototype was demonstrated in a bioscope shown at the Leicester Square cinema to the military attachés of all the embassies and legations in London, including the Germans, but Hornsby's sold their patent soon after. At the beginning of 1915 the First Lord of the Admiralty, Winston Churchill, wrote to Prime Minister Asquith with an idea for small, armoured, tracked vehicles. Foster's of Lincoln, who had been associated with the invention of a pre-War caterpillar tractor, were commissioned to carry out the experiments. The project was code-named 'Water carrier for Mesopotamia'. On 15 September 1916 the first of these 'water tanks' went into action on the Somme.

Those returning from the war were exhorted to help build a land fit for heroes. A war memorial was not high on the list of priorities. Three attempts were made to set up a fund, but it took until April 1922 to raise enough money. Circulars were delivered to every house in Lincoln by disabled ex-soldiers, lantern slides were screened at the Theatre Royal and Palace Theatre, and concerts were put on, as a result of which £3,200 was collected. The industrial and financial conditions in the city were against the war memorial project. A Lincoln Labour Party had been founded in 1907 by a band of working men who met in Danes Terrace. By 1913 they had a Labour man, Arthur Taylor, on the City Council. A tailor from Melville Street, he went on to be the first Labour MP for Lincoln in 1924, winning his seat from the Tories by 39 votes. In 1914 a second Labour councillor was elected. During the First World War the Dean of Lincoln, Dr T.C. Fry, and the Bishop, the pacifist and teetotal Dr Edward Hicks, worked with the local Labour Party agent to try, with small success, to make the unimaginative and reactionary City Council do something about housing for the crowds of workers who had flooded in to work in the munitions factories. Labour supporters from Lincoln took part in the Jarrow March. From 1945 until 1974 Labour controlled the City Council.

Times were bad for Lincoln's industries after the First World War, to some extent because of the loss of the Russian market as a consequence of the revolution and British support for the forces opposed to the Bolshevik regime. By 1923 Robey's order books were looking empty and men were laid off. Ruston and Hornsby were obliged to cut their workforce in Lincoln and Grantham from 13,000 to 4,750. Men spent their days polishing their machines and long queues formed at the Labour Exchange. To meet the crisis, Ruston's turned to motor car production. At the same time Colonel Ruston helped fund the development of a garden suburb called Swanpool, on low ground south-west of the city.

The Twentieth Century saw the rise and fall of the cinema. Originally Lincoln had eight. The Grand Electric opened in 1911 on the site of a hairdresser's at 262a High Street. It closed in 1960. By 1913 there were three cinemas — the Cinematograph Hall in the Corn Exchange, the Grand Electric and the Central Hall, originally called the Temperance Hall. In this same year the first film in colour, of the Royal visit to India and the Durbar, was shown at the Theatre Royal. The Regal started in a former grocery and provisions shop near the Stonebow in 1915 as The Picture House, seating 1,200. Renamed in 1931, its unique feature was its café-lounge, where patrons could watch the film while taking tea. It was closed in 1966. The Savoy opened in 1936 with Ronald Coleman and Basil Rathbone in *A Tale of Two Cities*. In the following year the Ritz opened its doors with *San Francisco*, starring Clark Gable and Spencer Tracey. A sign of the times, the Ritz provided parking for 250 cars. The Palace Theatre in Newland began as the Masonic Hall in 1871. The masons then sold the hall to the Conlan Brothers who presented stage shows, while the masons remained in part of the building. In 1901 the theatre was reopened as the Empire Music Hall by Councillor George Beagle, whose initials decorated the heavy, red, velvet curtains. Subsequently it became the Plaza Cinema, until it went up in flames in 1943.

A Lincoln City football team was playing in 1861 but it seems to have become defunct by the 1870s. The present City Football Club was founded in 1883, playing on a ground behind the High Street on land subsequently built up as Sibthorpe, Nelthorpe, and Abbott Streets. The Club moved to its Sincil Bank ground in 1884. It registered its first success in winning the Lincolnshire Senior Cup in 1888, '91 and '92, and eleven more times before 1939. It was also successful in the Midland League and the Football Alliance between 1889–1892 and, in the latter year, turned professional. Lincoln FC was one of twelve clubs originally selected to form the Second Division of the football League in 1892, remaining in this division until 1920. Thereafter Lincoln had to seek re-election and only regained League status in 1921 with the formation of Divison 3 (North). Since 1945 Lincoln City FC have fielded four promotion-winning teams — in 1947–8, 1951–2, 1975–6, and 1980–1.

From a two-mile course, the Lincolnshire Handicap had been reduced to a 'straight mile' in 1865, run at various times of the year. A century later, the Horse Race Betting Board decided not to allocate fixtures to Lincoln after 1965, and, despite appeals and protests, the last meeting took place on 20–21 May 1964 and the Handicap was transferred to Doncaster in 1966.

Following the 1944 Education Act, there was considerable expansion in education in Lincoln, especially during the 1960s. In 1958 the new Boultham Moor Girls' Secondary Modern School opened. Its domestic science block was particularly notable for its furnished flat, with rooms similar in area to those in Corporation houses. The new infants' school at Birchwood, opened in 1965, its classrooms each with their own toilets and washroom, and opening onto the central school hall, was considered ahead of its time. Other new schools opened or formed were SS Peter and Paul Secondary School (1957), Our Lady of Lincoln Junior (1963), Manor Leas (1968), the City School (moved from its Monks Road site in 1968), St Christopher's Special School (1969, replacing St Catherine's, founded in 1955), Yarborough Secondary Comprehensive (1970) incorporating St Francis School for the physically handicapped, St Giles Nursery School (1973) with a clinic and parents' workshop, and Lincoln Christ's Hospital School (1974) which combined Christ's Hospital School, the Girls' High School, Lincoln School, and St Giles and Myles Cross Schools into a new comprehensive school.

In 1974 Lincoln lost its independent status as a county borough. Its police force had already been merged into the Lincolnshire County Constabulary. Now its other functions, for example as an education authority, were taken into the new Lincolnshire County Council, which came into being as a result of local government reorganisation. The city became a district council, but the chair was allowed to retain the title of Mayor.

The late sixties was when conservation became a major issue. Local newspapers proclaimed a 'New look for Lincoln'. The Pelham Bridge flyover, a new telephone exchange, Co-op House, the Eastgate Hotel, and Danesgate House were among the buildings constructed in a few years. Not everyone welcomed the new look. Some of its critics held a mock funeral in the city centre to publicise their view that the new architecture was the death of Lincoln. Not only was most of the new building architecturally unacceptable, it involved the destruction of sites of historic and archaeological interest. In addition, many streets of still-serviceable small-scale Victorian housing, once occupied by those whose labours had underpinned the industrial city, were swept away.

One of the planning proposals which brought matters to a head (and may have led to a change of policy) was a scheme to make the traditional shopping area of Sincil Street on the edge of the covered market, into a shopping mall. After a public enquiry, this scheme was dropped. A new approach to planning was evidenced with the establishment in 1968 of the first conservation area, centred on the Bail and the Cathedral, containing 75 per cent of the city's surviving buildings of architectural or historic interest. After local government reorganisation in 1974 it was possible to feel the city's heritage was safe. In that year the 'pedestrianisation' of the High Street below the Stonebow was completed.

In 1973 the City's MP, Dick Taverne, split with his Party over his right to express views about Britain's entry into Europe, which were in conflict with the local branch. Taverne founded the Democratic Labour Party, which took control of the City Council. He retained his seat in a by-election in 1973 and again in the General Election, losing eventually to the official Labour candidate, Margaret Jackson, in 1974, ending speculation that a third force was emerging in British politics.

But Lincoln is not an introspective place. As early as 1932 tenuous links existed with Lincoln, Nebraska, USA and moves were made to develop twinning with Pietermaritzburg in South Africa (now recalled in street names on the Ermine Estate) in 1947 and with Tours in France in 1953. However, in 1969, official documents were signed to establish relations with Neustadt an der Weinstrasse in the Federal Republic of Germany, a town which received its municipal charter in 1275. Looking towards the Haardt Mountains on the west and the River Rhine on the east, Neustadt was named by Ludwig I of Bavaria 'blossoming Palatinate, garden of Germany'. The twin towns enjoy regular exchanges and one of the high spots of the year in Lincoln is the arrival of the Neustadt wine for the citizens to sample. Plans to establish links with the city of Tangshan in the Hebei province of China are also under consideration. The Anglican diocese of Lincoln is also twinned with its Catholic counterpart in Bruges in Belgium, while links also exist with Australia due to the county's association with the explorer Matthew Flinders.

ABOVE: Tarmacadam replaced wooden blocks after 1897. CENTRE: The 'corpulent mass', as Pevsner called it. BELOW: When this motor rally was held in the castle grounds no-one envisaged how the car would transform the shape of the city.

ABOVE: By 1910 traffic congestion was increasing in the city. BELOW:
The Brayford was still a working pool at the start of this century.

ABOVE: Before the First World War the Brayford was used for agricultural
cargoes. BELOW: The High Bridge and Waterside eighty years ago.

ABOVE: The Glory Hole, much renovated. BELOW: Probably one of the first planes seen in Lincoln, when it touched down on the West Common for fuel.

ОСТОРОЖНО
ПЕТРОГРАД
743

ABOVE: Little Willie, built at Fosters, Lincoln, the first prototype tank and BELOW: An early Mk 1 tank 'With care to Petrograd' to put German spies off the scent.

ABOVE: Three attempts were made to raise money for the War Memorial.
It was finally unveiled on 25 October 1922. BELOW: Part of the St Giles
Estate, some of the first council housing in Lincoln, built in the thirties.

131

ABOVE: Tram personnel 1914–15. BELOW: The old 'bus station, Lincoln,
a painting by Fred Lawson.

LEFT: Early twentieth expansion: New Boultham. RIGHT: St Giles Church, incorporating the former St Peter-at-Arches. BELOW: The Ritz 1937–81, reopened 1984. The first to offer deaf-aids to patrons.

ABOVE: The frozen Brayford in 1962. BELOW: Today the Brayford has lost much of its former commercial significance and functions as a marina. Around it stand the cliff-like blank-faced buildings of the new Lincoln.

ABOVE: The new look Waterside, east of the High Bridge. BELOW: Traditional Sincil Street remains, a compromise between conservation and development.

ABOVE: The new architecture: St John's church on the Ermine Estate.
BELOW: The Cathedral from Vicar's Court — a tranquil reminder of the
past.

136

The revival of the Lincoln Cycle of Mystery Plays by the Drama Department
of Bishop Grosseteste College, director Keith Ramsay.

Select Bibliography

General Histories

J.W.F. Hill's monumental *Medieval Lincoln, Tudor and Stuart Lincoln, Georgian Lincoln*, and *Victorian Lincoln* remain unsurpassed. The annual reports of The Trust for Lincoln Archaeology, subsequently and briefly subsumed into The Trust for Lincolnshire Archaeology, and now reorganised as The City of Lincoln Archaeological Unit are essential for anyone wishing to keep up-to-date on the progress of archaeological research in the city.

Roman and early Medieval Lincoln.

M.J. Jones, 'New Streets for Old', *Council for British Archaeology Report 59: Roman Urban Topography in Britain and The Western Empire*, ed. F. Grew and B. Hobley. 1985

M.J. Jones, 'Archaeology in Lincoln', *British Architectural Association Conference Transactions for 1982 VIII, Medieval Art and Architecture at Lincoln Cathderal*. 1986

E. Nurser ed., *Archaeology in Lincolnshire 1984–5*. 1985

Blackburn, C., Colyer, Dolley, *Early Medieval Coins from Lincoln and its shire*, Archaeology of Lincoln VI/1. Council for British Archaeology. 1983

Lincoln Cathedral

R. Gem, 'Lincoln Minster: Ecclesia Pulchra, Ecclesia Fortis', in *Medieval Art and Architecture at Lincoln Cathedral*, 1986, vide supra.

D.H. Farmer, *St. Hugh of Lincoln*, Darton, Longman, Todd. 1985

D.H. Farmer, *St. Hugh of Lincoln*, Bodleian Library Exhibition Catalogue. 1986

Houses

The Survey of Ancient Houses I and II, Lincoln Civic Trust 1984 and 1987, ed. S. Jones, K. Major and J. Varley

Medieval Drama in Lincoln

G. Wickham, *The Medieval Theatre*, Weidenfeld and Nicolson. 1984

The pre-Reformation Church in Lincoln

H. Salter, *Subsidy collected in the Diocese of Lincoln in 1526*, Oxford. 1909

R.W. Southern, *Robert Grosseteste*, OUP. 1986

The Medieval City

W.M. Ormrod ed., *England in the Thirteenth Century*, Proceedings of the 1984 Symposium at Harlaxton College, Grantham. 1985

E.W. Moore, *The Fairs of Medieval England*, The Pontifical Institute of Medieval Studies. 1985.

Figures in *italics* refer to illustrations

Index

Abbeys, priories, convents
Barlings 49
Friaries, Carmelites
(Whitefriars) 62,67
Dominicans
(Blackfriars) 62,79
Franciscans (Greyfriars)
... 38,62,67,78,88,111,112
Friars of the Sack 62
Knights of the Hospital of
St John, Eagle 50
La Grande
Chartreuse 36,37
St Catherine's Priory,
Lincoln 30,62
St Martin's, Sees 59
St Mary's, York 63,67
St Mary Magdalene, cell
of St Mary's York 63
Selby 60
Acts of Parliament
Catholic Emancipation,
1829 109
Elizabethan Poor
Law 78,85
Enclosure 96
Infectious Diseases,
Notification of 99
Municipal
Reform 87,109
Parliamentary Reform
1832 87
Statute of Artificers 78
Agemund the priest 59
aldermen 23,48,50,77,79,
81,97
Alexandria 16
Allsopp, Thomas 108
Amsterdam 80
Angevins 47
Anglian 22
apprentices 78,79,85,96
aquaduct 16
Arboretum, the 63,109,
110,*117*
Arles 21
armour, body 14
army, Roman 13
Arras, Simon of 50
Ashley's, glass and china
merchants 97
Asia Minor 16,21
Askeby, Walter de 72
Asquith, Herbert 123
Assembly Rooms 84,112
Atherstone Place 99
Atlantic 30,107
Audley, Erasmus 83
Australia 125
Avalon
William, sieur of 36
Anne of 36
Bacon, Roger 38
Bailiff, the Royal 23,47,48
Ball, Ann 79
Baltic 23
Banks, Sir Joseph 84
Lady 84
Banzo's, Professor,
performing dogs 110
Bargate, the Great 29,*52*
Barlow's, newsagents 98
Barlow, Mrs, confectioner 98
Basilica,
the Roman 14,15,22
baths, Roman 15

Bavaria 125
Beadle, bedell, the 48
of the Beggars 78
Beagle, Councillor
George 124
Beaumont, Fee 85,98
Henry de 30
Beckett (formerly Jackson),
Margaret MP 125
beggars 77,78
Bek, Anthony 70
Bellaset *57,72*
Belvoir Castle,
Leicestershire 27
Berry, Colonel 81
Beverley, Yorkshire 63
Bible, Hebrew 71
Bishops, Archbishops
Adelfius 21,22
Alexander of Blois,
'the Magnificent'
(1123–48) 36,60,70
Alnwick, William de
(1436–50) 70
Beaufort, Cardinal Henry
(1398–1405) 39
Burghersh, Henry
(1320–1342) 39,70
Canterbury, Archbishops
of 72,111
Chesney, Robert de
(1148–67) 70
Dalderby, St John de
(1300–1320) 39
Grosseteste, Robert
(1235–53) 36,37,38,
44,61,62,72
Hicks, Edward
(1910–20) 124
Hugh, St, of Lincoln (Hugo of
Avalon, 1186–1200) 30,
36,37,38,50,61,71
Hugh of Wells
(1209–1235) 30,70
Longland, John
(1521–47) 43,64,70
Neile, Richard
(1614–17) 70
Remigius, Remy of Fecamp
(1072–94) 35,36,38
Rotherham, Thomas
(1472–80) 70
Williams, John
(1642–1654) 70
Wolsey, Cardinal
Thomas (1514) 62
Wordsworth, Christopher
(1869–85) 112
Wulfig, Bishop of Mid-Anglia
and Lindsey 35
York, Archbishop of 38
Bishops' Palace,
the 70,73,80,81,109
Black Death, the 50,51
Black Prince, Edward the 39
Blecca 21,22
Blomfield, Sir A.B. 112
Sir Reginald 112,*118*
Bolton, Lancashire 85
Bordeaux 16
Borough Fund, the 97
Boston, Lincolnshire 49,50,
77,80,108

Boultham 28,99,123,*133*
Bracebridge 51,99,112,113
Heath 108,123
Branston 51
Brayford Pool 13,16,28,60,
64,85,*100,127,128,134*
Breslau 110
Bridges
Gowts 85
High Bridge *82,*85,96,
102,128
Pelham 125
Thornbridge *115*
Brigantes 15
Bristol 71
Britain 13,23
Bromhead, Mrs A.F. 99
Brooke, W.H. 108
Brough (*Crococalana*) 14
Brownlow, Lord 98
Broxtowe (*Margidunum*) 14
Bruges 49,125
Bucharest 110
Buckden,
Huntingdonshire 70,*73*
Budapest 110
Burghersh, Bartholomew 39
Burial Board 98
Burley, William 96
Burton 51
and Proctor,
millwrights 109
burwarmot, the 23,24,47,50
Byrd, William 69,77
Cadwallder, Prince 28
Cambridgeshire 13
canabae 14
Canons, Austin 36,60
Canterbury 27,38
Canwick, Lincolnshire 51
Car Dyke 16
carbatina 19
Carthusians 36
Casterton,
Northamptonshire 30
Castle .... 23 passim *32,33,102,126*
bailey, the 27,*31,*35,71
Barbican, the 29
Cobb Hall 29,*34,103*
Ditch 27,29
Lucy Tower 27,28,29,*104*
Market in Castle
ditch 29,49
motte 27,28
Castleford Canal,
Leeds 107,108
Cathedral,
(Minster) .... 13 passim,
39,42,94
Angel Choir *39,42,*58
Bayeux, Constitution of
Cathedral of 35
Bounegarth 70
canons 35,36,38,39,63,69,79
'cathedra' (throne) 39
central tower 38,39,113
Chancellor 36
chapels *104*
St John the Baptist 38,39
St Mary Magdalen *41,*66
Chapter 36,69,72
Cross 47
House 29,36,*45,*63

choir 36,*41,*61
close wall *45,*69
Cook, Canon,
Subdean 36,38
Dean ... 36,63,64,69,*74,*79,124
Dean and Chapter 40,43,
47,69,72,79,83,87
Easter Sepulchre 61
evensong 36
fabric fund *40,*70
frieze *44*
Galilee Porch 38,61
Green 83
Judgement Porch 39,*49*
matins 36
Minster Yard 35,*41,*
74,77,80,87,*89,91*
Morning Chapel 36
Nave 36,38
Noiers, Geoffrey de 37,38
Precentor 35,69
Priest Vicars 38
Rouen, Constitution of
Cathedral of 35
St Mary's Guild 37
School 79
shrine of St Hugh 39,*40,*
*58,*60,61,64,70,71
spires 83
Subdean 69,*74*
Treasurer 36,64
Vicars' Court *43,*70,*136*
Wren Library 98
cats 24
cattle, cows and oxen 24,29
cattle market *115*
Cause, William 49
cemeteries 98
Census of Religious
Worship, 1851 96,112
centurion 14
century 14
Cerialus, Quintus
Petillius 14
Chancellor Benson 111
Chancery, the 70,*74*
Chartists 108
Chateau Gaillard 37
Chatterton's, bakers 97
Cherry Willingham,
Lincolnshire 51
Cheshire 28
Chest Clinic 98
Chester 15,23
Earl Ranulf of 28
China 23,125
Christ 61,71
Christians, early 21,22
churches and chapels
All Saints-in-the-Bail 59
All Saints in Hungate 60
Baptists 85
Celtic 22
Free Methodist,
Silver Street 85
Holy Trinity and St John .. 60
Holy Trinity and
St Margaret 60
Holy Trinity-below-Hill 60
Independent Chapel .. 85,*105*
of England 22,29,62,85
Presbyterian 85
Roman Catholic 22,29,
38,125
St Augustine 59
St Bartholomew 60
St Bavons 72
St Benedict (St Bene't) of

139

Wigford 60,*66*,77,81,113
St Clement 60
St Cuthbert-in-the-
    Bullring 49
St Edmund 60
St Faith-in-Newland 60
St George 60
St Helen 60
St John-in-Newport
    .... 49,60,*66,67*,80
St John's Roman Catholic
    Church 112
St Lawrence 60,78,84
St Margaret-in-
    Pottergate 60,78
St Mark 16,60,96,112
St Martin ... 60,86,*89*,110,112
St Martin-in-the-
    Dernstall 60
St Mary 'Crakepool' 60
St Mary-le-Wigford 59,60,
    62,*65*,79,95,112
St Mary Magdalene 36,81
St Michael-on-the-Mount
    .... 59,*65*,72,81
St Nicholas 60,95,*105*,113
St Paul-in-the-Bail
    22,59,112
St Paulinus *24*
St Peter-at-Arches 59,60,
    79,87,*89*,110,112,113,*133*
St Peter-at-Gowts 59,60,
    65,78,85,98,111
St Peter-at-Pleas
    (ad Placita) 23,59,60
St Peter-at-the-Wells
    (at-the-Spring) 59
St Peter-in-Eastgate ... 72,78,
    80,*87*,112
St Peter 'Stanthaket' 60
St Rumbold 60
St Stephen-in-Midhergate
    (Newland) 60
St Swithin 78,95,112
Society of Friends
    Meeting House 85
Thomas Cooper Memorial
    Baptist Church 112
Zion Chapel 85
Churchill, Winston S. 123
City
    Bailiff................. 30,49,50,51
    cap of maintenance 47,
        48,*54*
    Common Council 64,84
    Seal *55*
    constable 77
    Corporation 77,78,79,84,
        87,96,97,111,113
    plate 87
    Council 87,99,111,
        123,124,125
    civic insignia 87
    Football Club 124
    gaol *91*
    mace 47,48,*54*
    Mayor .... 23 passim
    Mayor's chair *56*,87
    mootstone 23,50,60
    Provosts 48
    Sheriff 28,29,30,47,48,
        78,87
    sergeant-at-mace 47,48
    Sessions House 62
    swords 47,48,*54,56*
    sword-bearer 47,48
    Waits *55*,77
    wards 77

City News Room 112
Civil War 36,48,70,77,80
Clark, Philip, labourer 80
Clarkson, Elizabeth 73
    William 96
Claypole Mill 85
Clayton 108,109,110,123
Clifford's Tower, York 71
Clipstone, Nottinghamshire
    30
Cockerill, Matthew, glass
    and china merchants 97
cohort 14
coins, coinage 13,22,23,*26*
Colchester
    (*Camulodunum*) 14,15
Coleman, John 84,124
colonia 14,15
colonists, American 48
Colony, Chartist 108
Colsuen 59
Common Prayer, Book of 62
conduit 79
conservation area 125
Cook, Captain James 84
Co-op House 125
Cooperative Society,
    Lincoln 110,111,*116*
Coritani (or Coritavi) 13
Corn Exchange 97,108,
    110,111,112,124
County
    Court 29,85
    Gaol 29,86,95,97,108
    News Room 112
crake 60
Crècy, battle of 39
Crewe and Sprague,
    architects 84
Cromwell, Oliver 80
    Thomas 48,63
Cross, Queen Eleanor 30,
    58,81
Crossby, Edmund 96
Crown Court 29
Crystal Palace 110
Culloden, battle of 83
Cumberland 72,78
Danelaw, the 23,27
Danesgate House 125
Dauphiné, the 36
Decuriones 15
defences, Roman 14,15,16,21
Defoe, Daniel 59,83,85
Denmark 21
Deuteronomy, The Book of .. 71
Dickens, Charles 109
diocese 21,22,35,37,61,125
Dispensary, the Lincoln 98
dogs 24
Domesday Book, Domesday
    Survey, the 23,35,50,59,60
Doncaster, Yorkshire 124
Dorchester-on-Thames,
    Oxfordshire 35
Doughty, Mr, ropemaker 85
Drake, Nathan 92
Drinsey Nook,
    Lincolnshire 99
Dubrovnik 38
Duckering, Charles 109
duumviri 15
East Anglia 14
    Gate 16,*18*,70
    Stoke (*Ad Pontem*) 14
Edison, Joseph 110
Eirtag 59
Ellison, Richard 107

Ermine Estate, the *136*
Essex 13
Exchange Buildings 108
Exodus, The Book of 71
Eynsham, Oxfordshire *26*
Fabian 14
fairs and markets 49,51,*106*
    Boston Fair 49
    butchery 96
    Buttermarket 84,96,112
    fish market 96
    Horse Fair 97
    Newport 49,69
    St Ives Fair 49
    Stall 97
    Winchester 49
'Fair of Lincoln', battle of 29
Farmery, Dr John 80
Feasts
    Corpus Christi 49,61
    Holy Cross 48
    Purification 28
    St Anne 49
    St Hugh 51
Fecamp, Normandy 35
fens 13,87
Fields and Commons
    Carholme 28,80,84
    Cow Paddle 98
    Dalderby Close (Tower
        Close) 79
    Kennington 108
    Long Leas 80
    Monks Leys 63,109
    Newport Close 79
    South Common 30,62,
        81,98,109
    Swine Green 30
    West Common 28,80,
        97,123,*129*
Fiskerton, Lincolnshire 13,51
Fitz-Gilbert, Baldwin, Lord
    of Clare 28
Flanders 49
Flavia Caesariensis 16
Flavinus, Lucius
    Sempronius 14
Fleming, John the 50
Fletcher's, butchers 98
Flinders, Matthew 125
Ford's, greengrocery 98
fortifications,
    Roman 14,15,16
    forum, the Roman 15,*18*,22
    Foss Dyke 16,28,79
Foster, William 109
Fotherby, William 96
fountain, Roman 15
Fowler, C. Hodgson 112
France 16,48,72,125
freemen 23,47,49,50,78,87
French army, the 29
Frescobaldi, Emery de 30
Frontinus, C. Antistus 15
Fry, Dr T.C., Dean of
    Lincoln 124
Gadsby, George 96
Gainsborough,
    Lincolnshire 80,83,86,95
Garewic 59
Gas Works 110
Gaul 16,21
Gaunt, John of 39,69,70,*88*
Germany 16,21,125
Gilbert, Lizzie 110
gildhall 51
gild merchant 50
Gilds 78

Gloucester 15,71
    Earl of 28,38
Godric 59
Gospel, according to
    St Luke 71
    St Mark 61
    St Matthew 61
grain 24,29,77,78,79
Grangershouse 79
Great Tom 87
    Exhibition, the 107,109
Greetwell, Lincolnshire 51
Greetwell Farm 107
Grimsby Dock 48
Guards, Irish Dragoon,
    The band of 107
Haardt Mountains,
    Germany 125
Halifax, Yorkshire 63
Hanging Bowl, the
    Lincoln 22,*25*
Harby, Nottinghamshire 30
Harpswell, Lincolnshire 80
Harrison, Mr, butcher,
    Dunholme 108
Hauser, Eustace le 50
Hawksford and Kirby,
    drapers 98
Haye, Nicholaa de la 28,29
    Robert de la 28
Hebei Province, China 125
Heraclea 14
Herbert, William 83
Hereford 23
hirings 78
Holy Rood Day 78
Hornsby 123,124
Horse Race Betting
    Board 124
horses 24,29
Hospitals and Nursing Homes
    Bromhead, The 99
    County 90,*93*,95,98,99,*119*
    Holy Innocents
        (Malandry) 61,*64*
    The Lawn 60,86,*90*
    Long Leys 99
    Red House 99
    St Bartholomew 72
    St Giles 62
Hotham, Sir John 80
House of Industry 85,86
Howard, John 86
Hudson, George 96, 107
Hull, Yorkshire 79,80,107
Humber Estuary,
    the 15,21,27
Hungary 16
husbandmen 78
Iceni 14
Inns and Hotels
    Angel 84,*89*
    Black Boy 83
    Black Goat 98
    Cardinal's Hat 62,*81*
    City Arms 98
    Eastgate 125
    Green Dragon 108
    Harlequin 83,*90*
    Pyewipe 108
    Three Horse Shoes,
        Waddington 84
    Wig and Mitre 73
insulae 15
Iron Age, the *12*,13
Irving, Washington 85
Italian bankers 30
Italy 16

Jarrow March 124
jersey knitting and
  spinning 78
Jews, the, of Lincoln 38,*56*,
            70,71,72
  Aaron *57*,70,72
  Court *58*
  Leo 60
  Jopin 71
Johannesburg, South
  Africa 110
'Joust of Lincoln', the
  battle of 28,36
Kent 72
Kesteven 13
Kings and Queens
  Albert, Prince 48
  Anne Boleyn 62
  Boudicia 14
  Catherine of Aragon 62
  Catherine Howard 70
  Charles I 30,48,80
  Edgar 23
  Edward the Confessor 27
  Edward I 29,30,38,72
  Edward II 29,30,49
  Edward III 49,51
  Eleanor of Castile 30,38,
            39,50,81
  Elizabeth I 62,64,72,86
  Henry I 60,71
  Henry II, of Anjou 28,30,
        36,37,49,50,70,72
  Henry VII 48
  Henry VIII 62,63,64,70
  James I 70,84
  John 28,30,38,48
  Ludwig I, of Bavaria 125
  Mary I Tudor 77
  Matilda 28
  Richard I, Coeur de
    Lion 37,47,48,71
  Richard II 48,50
  Richard III 48,51
  Stephen 28,*31*,36,47,70
  William I, the Conqueror
    · 27,28,37
  William III, of Orange 48
  William of Scotland 38
knights 23,27,28,35,36,37
knitting 85,86
Krakow 110
Labour Party 123,124,125
Lancaster
  Duchy of 29,87
  Earl of 29
Lancaster Herald 63
land-gable 23
land toll penny 72
Lawmen 23
Laxton, Nottinghamshire 27
Leeds Model Band 110
Legbourne, Peter of 70
legion, Roman 13,14
Legion d'Honneur 110
legionary fortress 14,15
Leland, John 64,79
liberties 30
libraries 30,98,111,112
Lilipudlian Ladies, Lizzie
  Gilbert's troup of 110
limestone 13,14,15
Lincoln .... 11,*12*,13 passim, *53*,
  54,*88*,*93*,100,114,121,126,*132*
  Campanologium 110
  City and County
    Museum 13,62
  Club 112

Corn Exchange and
  Market Company 97
  County of 51
  Green 49
  Handicap 84,124
  Rifle Corps 110
  Scarlet 49
Lincolnshire .... 27 passim
  County Constabulary 125
  County Council 125
Lincolnshire Rising,
  the 62,63,64,70
Lindum .... 13,14,15,*20*,21̕,22
  Colonia 15,16,21
Little, Mrs, milliner 98
London 23,30,47,63,77,
    84,85,87,108,123
Lunaris, Marcus Aurelius 15
Lunatic Asylum,
  County 86,98,*119*
Macedonia 14,16
Magna Carta 30,*34*,48
mail, Lincoln to Hull 107
Mainz 15
Malmesbury, William of 59
Manchester, Earl of 80
Map, Walter 37
Marett, William 78
Market Rasen,
  Lincolnshire 99
Marston Moor, battle of 80
Masada 71
Massachusetts, USA 69
  Governor of 69
McDouall, Dr Peter
  Murray 108
Mechanics Institute 111,112
Medical Officer of Health 99
Meers, Sir Thomas 79
Mercia, Earl Leofric of 59
Metham, George, 'cycle
  fitter 98
Midland Football League ... 124
Mint 23
  Wall 15,*17*
Moigne, Thomas 63
Monson, Mr Justice 79
Morcar, Earl 59
murage 23
Murray, John .... 83̕
Mystery plays, Lincoln
  Cycle of 61,*137*
National Land Company ... 108
Netherlands 21
Neustadt am der
  Weinstrasse 125
Newark-on-Trent,
  Nottinghamshire 27,80
Newcastle, Earl of 80
Newland Gate *53*
Newport Arch 14,*17*,29
newspapers
  Hull and Lincolnshire
    Chronicle 83
  Lincoln Gazette 83
    Gazetteer *83*
    Journal 83
  Rutland, and Stamford
    Mercury 83, 108
  Lincolnshire Chronicle 95,
            99, 108
Nield, Mr 86
Ninth (IX) Legion, the
  Hispana 13,14,15,*17*,27
Normandy 27,37,59
Normans 16,23,27,35
Northampton 30,47
Northamptonshire 37

Northumbria 21
Norwich 23,27,71
Nottingham 27,59,107
  Sheriff of 49
Oberammergau 61
O'Connor, Feargus, MP 108
Odessa 110
ordo, the 15
Outi 59
Oxford 62
  University 62
Papal Interdict 38
Parham, Lord Willoughby
  of 80
Paris 37
  Exhibitions, 1878, 1900 ... 110
Parker, C.T., grocery and
  provisions merchant 97
Parliament 80,81
Peachy, John, plumber 80
Pepperdine, Joseph 108
Peters, J.A. 123
  Flying Machine designed
    by 123
  photographer 98
Pietermaritzburg 125
pigs 24,29
Pilgrimage of Grace, the 62
pillory 77
Pinfold 79
Plague 78
Plautius, Aulus 13
Poitou, Earl Roger of 59
Poldhu 110
ponderator 50
Pope
  Alexander 35
Population 24,27
Potter Hanworth,
  Lincolnshire 79,99
Pottergate Arch *45*
Poynton, Walter de, of
  Canwick 72
Praefectus 22
Prague 110
Prial Brook, the 99
principia 14,15
Pugin 85,*101*,112
Pump, Roman 16
Races, Lincoln 84,97
Railway, the Great
  Northern 96,97,99,107,108
  The Midland 99,107
Red Hall Estate 108
reservoirs
  Hartsholme 99
  Roman 16
Rest, The *76*
Revesby, Lincolnshire 84
Rhineland 14,16
Richthofen, Baron von 123
Ridings 23
Rivers
  Nene 14,16
  Rhine 125
  Thames 13
  Trent 14,16,21,50
  Witham ..... *12*,13 passim, *115*
Robertson, Thomas
  Shaftoe 83,84
Robey, Robert 109
  seaplane 123
Robin Hood 49
  Rifles 110
Roman emperors
  Constantine 21
  Diocletian 16,21
  Domitian 15

Hadrian 15,16
Julius Caesar 13
Nero 14
Roman Empire 14,15,16
Rouen, Ralf of 50
Roumare, William de 28
Royal Agricultural
  Show 107,123
  Engineers 110
Royalists 80,81
Rudgard, E.W.R. 107,108
Runnymede 30
Ruston, Joseph 109,110
Ryther, Mrs 79
St Albans, Hertfordshire 72
St Andrew's Hall 69
St Anne's Guild 61,77
St Giles estate 112,*131*
St Ives, Huntingdonshire 49
St Mary's Conduit 79,99
  Guildhall *68*,69
Saints
  Alban 21
  Augustine 21
  Bernard of Clairvaux 36
  Francis of Assisi 36
  Gilbert of Sempringham ... 62
  Paul 21,22
  Paulinus 22
  Thomas à Becket 36,38
Salisbury, Wiltshire 62
Sanfeius, Gaius 14
Scandinavia 23
schools
  Birchwood Infants 125
  Bishop Grosseteste
    College of HE *105*
    King Elementary 111
  Boultham Moor Girls
    Secondary 124
  grammar 79,87,112
  Lincoln Christs
    Hospital 86,125
    City School 111,*121*,125
  Manor Leas Junior 125
  Monks Road Junior 111
  Myle Cross Secondary 125
  National, Westgate *120*
  Night School 111
  Our Lady of Lincoln RC
    Junior 125
  Rosemary Lane 111
  SS Peter & Paul RC
    Secondary 125
  St Christopher's
    Special 125
  St Francis 125
  St Giles Nursery 125
    Secondary 125
  School of Science and
    Art 111
  Skellingthorpe 111
  Spring Hill 111
  Victoria Infants' 111
  Wesleyan 111
  Yarborough Secondary
    Comprehensive 125
Scotland 29,96
Second (II) Legion,
  Adiutrix 15
  Senecio, Aurelius 15
  Serverus, Babudius 14
  sevir augustalis 15
Sharpe, John,
  confectioner 98
Sheaf ironworks 109
sheep 24,29
Shelford, Nottinghamshire ... 60

Sherwood, Forest of 49,70
shire 23
shops 14,15,49,51,96,*102*,107
shrines 15
Shuttleworth 108,109,
110,123
Sibthorp, Col Charles de
Laet Waldo 109
Siford the priest 60
signifier 14
Simnel, Lambert 48
Sincil Dyke *100,101*
Siward the priest 60
Skellingthorpe,
Lincolnshire 86,99
Solent, Estuary of 21
Somerby, Richard 79
Sopwith *Camel* 123
Sowerby's, pork
butcher 97,98
Spafford, J. 98
Spain 13,14,16
spinning 85,86
springs 16
Squire, George 96
Staffordshire 27
stalls 49,96,*106*
Stanham, Stephen of 49
Staple 50
Mayor of 50
steelyard 50
Stark, Adam 83
steam engine, portable 109
Stewart, Charles 108
Stoke by Newark 48
Stoke Newington,
Buckinghamshire 84
Stonebow *4,23,55,62,78,*
*79,86,96,122,*124,125
Stow, Lincolnshire 28,*68*
streets, lanes, and roads
Abbot Street 124
Alderman's Walk 123
Bail, the ... 29,*76,*85,86,87,125
Bailgate 14,15,85,112
Bank Street 85
Brant Road *116*
Briggate 60,79
Broadgate 69,98,112,*118*
Burley's Row 96
Canwick Road 109
Carholme 98,110
Castle Hill 83,112
Square *91,103*
Clasketgate 85
Cornhill 96,97,98
Coultham Street 123
Danes Terrace 72,112,123
Dernstall 71
Eastgate 14
Elder Lane 95,96,97
Ermine Street 13,14,16,
50,60,69,125
Flaxengate (*Haraldstigh*)
.... 22,23,24,*25,*69,72
Fosse Way 14,16,50,69
Free School Lane 112
Grantham Lane 95
Grantham Street
(*Brancegate*) ... 22,23,72,111
Great North Road 50
Greestone, the *26*
Terrace 70
Guildhall Street ......,..... 98,112
High Street 29,60,62,69,
83,85,95,96,97,*102,*107,*113,*
113,*114,122,*124,125
Hungate 30,60

James Street 69
Jobbers Road 95
Lindum Hill 86
Terrace 98
Michaelgate 15,23,60,69
Mikelgate 23,60,79
Mint Street 98
Monks Lane 79,97
Road ... 63,98,110,111,112,
115,116
Nelthorpe Street 124
Nettleham Road 99
Newland (see also suburbs)
.... 30,60,73,79,85,111
Newport (see also suburbs)
.... 62,69,79,80,98,111
New Road 86
Nixon's Court 95,96
Pottergate 70
St Bene't's Square 112
St Mary's Street 112
Saltergate 60,86
Sibthorpe Street 124
Silver Street 85,98,110,
111,112
Sincil Bank 59,124
Street 95,96,97,98,
125,*135*
Steep Hill 69
Strait, the 73,79,*81,*86
Tillbridge Lane 16
Tolbothe Lane 79
Waterside 69,85,95,96,
98,*135*
West End 98
Parade 30
street system, Roman 14,15,
21,23
Stuff Ball, the 84,85
Subsidy Rolls, 1332, 1526 ... 51
suburbs
Bagholme 59
Butwerk 69
Carholme 98
Mile Cross 63
Newland 30,60,73,79,
85,111
Newport 62,69,79,80,
98,111
Stamp End 62
West End 112
Wigford 22,60,62,69
Suffolk
Duchess of 77
Duke of 63
Sutherland, Duke of 110
Sutton Hoo burial ship 22
Swinderby Moor,
Lincolnshire 50
Swynford, Katherine 39,70
Taillebois, Countess Lucy
de 28
Tallis, Thomas 77
Tangshan, China 125
Taverne, Dick, MP 125
Taverner, John 77
Taylor, Councillor Arthur,
MP 123
telephone exchange 125
Temple Gardens 107,109
Tennyson, Lord Alfred
statue of 98,*118*
theatres and cinemas
Central, the 124
Cinematographic Hall,
the 124
Empire Music Hall, the ... 124
Grand Electric, the 124

Palace Theatre,
the 123,124
Picture House, the 124
Plaza, the 124
Regal, the 124
Ritz, the 124,*133*
Savoy, the 124
Theatre Royal, the 83,84,
123,124
Theological College,
the 111,*121*
threshing machine 108
Tochi 59
tombstones *18*
Tooley, Mr of Boston 80
Torksey, Lincolnshire 29,
50,107
Tours, France 125
Tower of London 64
trades and industries
actors 50
archers 50
bakers 49
barbers 50
brewers 49,73,99,107,108
brickmakers 85,95,108
brush-maker 98
chimney sweep 98
clothiers 49,78,79
clothmill 77
confectioners 98
cutlers 98
'cycle fitter 98
drapers 98
dyers, dyehouse 50,77
founderers,
foundries 73,108
fullers 50
glass and china
merchants 23
greengrocery 98
grocers 98,124
jewellers 23,98
leatherworkers and
cordwainers 79
maltsters, malting 23,86,
107,108
masons and stonemasons
.... 50,108
mercers 50
metalworkers,
metalworking 23,78,79
milliner 98
minstrels 50
newsagents 98
pork butcher 98
potters, potteries 16,49
ropemaker, ropery 85
sailors 50
skinners 73
tailors 123
tilers 50
umbrella-makers 98
weavers 50,77
Turner, J.M.W. *94*
typhoid 99,123
Usher, Gallery 109,112
James Ward 112
Val d'Isère, France 36
Valerius, Gaius 14
Varty, Jonathan, pork
butcher 98
Veale's, builders 84
via
praetoria 14
principalis 14
sagularis 14
Vienna 110

Vikings, Danish 22,23
Waddington, Lincolnshire ... 51
Wales, Gerald of 37
Walker, George 96
walls 15,16,23,27,*46,*70
Wallingford, Oxfordshire 72
wapentakes 23,63
War 1914–18 98,124
Memorial 123,*131*
Warren, Charles 98
Warwick, Earl of 38
Washingborough,
Lincolnshire 13,51
Water Newton
(*Durobrivae*) 22
water supply, Roman 16
weights and measures,
Assay of 29
Wells, Joseph 110
Welton, Lincolnshire 79,84
Wesley, John 85
Wessex 35
West Gate, the Roman 16,*19,*
29,*31*
lower city *20*
upper city *17,52*
Riding 107
Westmoreland 78
Whichcote, Square 80
Wickenby, William of 49
Willoughby,
Nottinghamshire 99
Wilson, George, chimney
sweep 98
Winceby, Battle of 80
Winchester, Hampshire 23
Windsor, Berkshire 35
Witham, Somerset 36,37,50
Wombwell's Menagerie 107
Woodstock, Royal Palace of,
Oxfordshire 37
York (*Eboracum, Jorvik*) ... 15,23,
27,38,62,71,79,85
Yorkshire 27,78
Young Men's Christian
Association (YMCA) 112
Ypres, Belgium (Flanders) ... 49
Zeppelin 123

Subscribers

Presentation Copies

1 The City of Lincoln
2 Lincolnshire County Council
3 The Dean & Chapter, Lincoln Cathedral
4 Bishop Grosseteste College
5 Beaumont Fee Education Centre
6 Cllr J.S. Robertson

7 Ian Beckwith
8 Clive & Carolyn Birch
9 David N. Robinson
10 Albert Ernest Bailey
11 Mrs B. Ferron
12 A.J. Gadd
13 C.J. Lester
14 J.J. Prewett
15 T.M. Blackburn
16 John Best
17 Mrs I. Weston
18 Mrs M.M. Whatmough
19 J. Peatfield
20 D. & E. Ballard
21 Lucy Anne Moss
22 G.S. Meanwell
23 Miss R. Tinley
24 Mrs J. Cornwell
25 S. Warmoth
26 Brogden & Co
27 Mrs S.M. Thornalley
28
29 N.J. Camamile
30 D.A. Brown
31 Christine Beckwith
32 Keith Beckwith
33 Clare Beckwith
34 Christ & Alice Metherell
35 Mary Phillips
36 Julian Morton
37 T.A. Cook
38 Salt Lake City Family
   History Library
39 Victoria & Albert
   Museum
40 London Guildhall
   Library
41 Howard E. Bicknell
42 Drury J. Whiteley
43 John Gregory
44 Keith Ramsay
45 Richard S. Eyre
46 Bob Shirley
47 Sibthorpe Library,
   Bishop Grosseteste
50 College
51 John Broughton
52 Olivia Kersey

53 G.B. Gould
54 K. Bradford
55 G.W. Lancaster
56 Mrs J. Clugston
57 Catherine Mary
   Sanderson
58 Colin G. R. Booth
59 Mrs N. Strong
60 G.B. Pacey
61 Tim Cartwright
62 Lincolnshire Library
126   Service
127 John H. Warner
128 R. Lansdall-Welfare
129 J.K. Thorpe
130 Colin A. Cornish
131 F.T. Baker OBE, FSA
132 Brian Borrill
133 Brian L. Ebb
134 Mrs J. M. Barlow
135 F.C. Bramwell
136 Pamela A. Crisp Beard
137 Bernard Fairfax
138 R.C. Atterby
139 John Anthony
140 Winston Kime
141 Mrs Margaret Birbeck
142 John Pountney
143 P.T. Bayley
144 Mrs Isabel Bailey
145 Frederick Cant
146 Andrew King
147 J.M. Overton MA
148 Rev C.H. Overton MA
149 K.W. Overton BA
150 J. Turner
151 Dr F. Henthorn
152 A.E. B. Owen
153 S.J.M. Dawes
154 G.W. Dunham
155 H.J. Atkinson
156 Edith Mary Boulton
157 Neil Richard Wright
158 Rosemary M. Oliver
159 Patrick Cormack
160 Frederick Wilham
   Spencer
161 John Russell Ingamells

162 Ian & Pat Walters
163
164 J.M. Walker
165 F.W. & M.J. Marston
166 E.T.S. Simpson
167 J.M. Dobson
168 Rev William Leary
169 Mrs Joan Herbert
170 Christopher C. Hunt
171 Miss J.E. Skinner
172 M.I. Needham
173 Carol Johnson
174 Ken Denniss
175 Lucy Eileen Cussons
176 Robert Dukes
177 F.C. Spillard
178 John K. Marfleet
179 Allan G. Parkin
180 W.G.M. Dickinson
181 J.F. Hinton
182 Mabel Reeson
183 John William Bee
184 David S. Jones
185 Charles & Yvonne
   Heward
186 Monks Dyke High
   School, Louth
187 Barry Young
188 R. Sellers
189 David G. Boulton
190 Chris Dobson
191 K. Ashton
192 Barbara Borman
193 Anthony J. Dent
194 K.P. Hutchinson
195 F.L. Stephenson
196 Miss J. Greetham
197 B. Ruffell-Ward
198 N.A.N. Sharpley
199 Pius Stampfli
200 John Burrows
201 P.M. Dear
202 E.G. Collyer
203 S.M. Stubbs
204 The Venerable David
   Leaning
205 M. Holmes
206 D. Bristow

207 Lenna M. Gore
208 Mrs W. Hardesty
209 Guy Gibbs
210 E. Hudson
211 Mrs Brenda Cannon
212 Mrs Joyce C. Leeman
213 Roderick Murdoch
214 Donald Amos
215 Colin Stones
216 R.W. Dales
217 Mary Poole
218 John Colbeck
219 Miss K.D. Venables
220 Chris Rose
221 Kathleen Major
222 Patrick Cormack MP
223 Mrs C.A. Bonny
224 A.J. Atkinson
225 Lincolnshire Archives
   Office
226 James & Barbara Kent
227 Thomas H. Chafer MA
228
229 Valerie Elizabeth Hope
230 R.B. Kealey
231 Canon Rex Davis
232 Helen Jennings
233 Rev D.F. Boutle
234 David Farrow
235 Edith Norah Wood
236 Mrs Jane M. Davey
237 G.W. Lauder
238 R.E. Dickinson
239 Museum of
   Lincolnshire Life
240 Mrs B. Ablett
241 Miss R.W. Larder
242 Norman Goy
243 Neil Richard Wright
244 J.H. John Peet
245 M.W. Codd
246 Maureen Blakey
247 Malcolm G. Knapp
248 Mrs Jean Murray
249
250 Miss Madge Hewson
251
252 Mrs M.C. Wallis

253 Delia Montlake
254 Peter N. Snowdon
255 Mrs Kathleen Hix
256 Mrs Shelia E. Waller
257 Patricia Larder
258 Mrs Joan Barnard
259 M.J. Jones MA, FSA, MIFA
260 J.K. Shaw
261 The Bishop of Lincoln
262 Philip B. Irving
263 William Hall & Mrs Olive Hall
264 Arthur Colin Crust
265 Frank Wood
266 Librarian, University
267 of Nottingham
268 Brenda M. Laviolette
269 H.J. Houghton
270 M.G. Kitchen
271 E. Hudson
272 Dr John B. Manterfield
273 Rev Harry Waite
274 G.H. Prestage
275 Gwen Schrimshaw
276 Thomas William Bee
277 John G. Handford
278 Susan Davies

279 J. Gray
280 Colin Stephen Tyson
281 M. Chantrey
282 Frederick Baker
283 Richard Marriott
284 Lincoln Post Express, Ontario
285 Mr & Mrs K. Dart
286 Mr & Mrs P. Doyle
287 Mr & Mrs G.R. Bennett
288 P. Graham
289 Wold School of English, Lincolnshire
290 R.A. Claridge
291 R.G. Mitchell
292
293 D.F. Smith
294 P.J. Rhodes
295 Jack Hardy
296 Jean A. Larson
297 Susan Dawson
298 A.C. Smith
299 I. McNish
300 Pearl Wheatley
301 Miss E.T. Wagstaffe
302 R. Willis
303 Mrs R.M. Hibbs

304 John G. Adams
305 Huntcliff Comprehensive School
306 Jacob D. Garonzhki
307 S. Waller
308 D. Wilkinson
309 F.C. Moats
310 J.S. Esberger
311 F.G. Felstead
312 Carol M. Dring
313 David Kaye
314 Allan Pearson
315 Miss K. Jankowski
316 K.R.W. Dand
317 S.A. Brignull
318 H.C. Grant
319 Rev & Mrs C.M.H. Frere
320 B.G. Cook
321 Jack Alexander Baird
322 S.H. Allen
323 Keith William Darwin
324 Susan Watkin
325 A.R. Howlett
326 Richard D.H. Wardell
327 R.B. Turrell
328 J. Chadwick

329 Mr & Mrs B.V. & E. Sleight
330 Charles Albert Brumby
331 Mrs B. Cannon
332 Anne Kay
333 J.E. Sharp
334 Tom Atkinson
335 Mrs Jean Pritchard
336 Helen Hampson
337 Agnes Mary Thacker
338 Linda Tilbury
339 F.W. Pearce
340 Pauline Ann Atkins
341 M. Joy Evans
342 Lincolnshire Library
344 Service
345 Humberside County
362 Libraries
363 John Turner
364 Douglas Pearman
365 John R. Ketteringham
366 John Bannister
367 George Baines
368 Dr Basil Weir
369 D.A. Olivant

Remaining names unlisted

ENDPAPERS — FRONT: From Speed's 1610 plan of Lincoln and BACK:
OS map of Lincoln and the surrounding area, 1824.

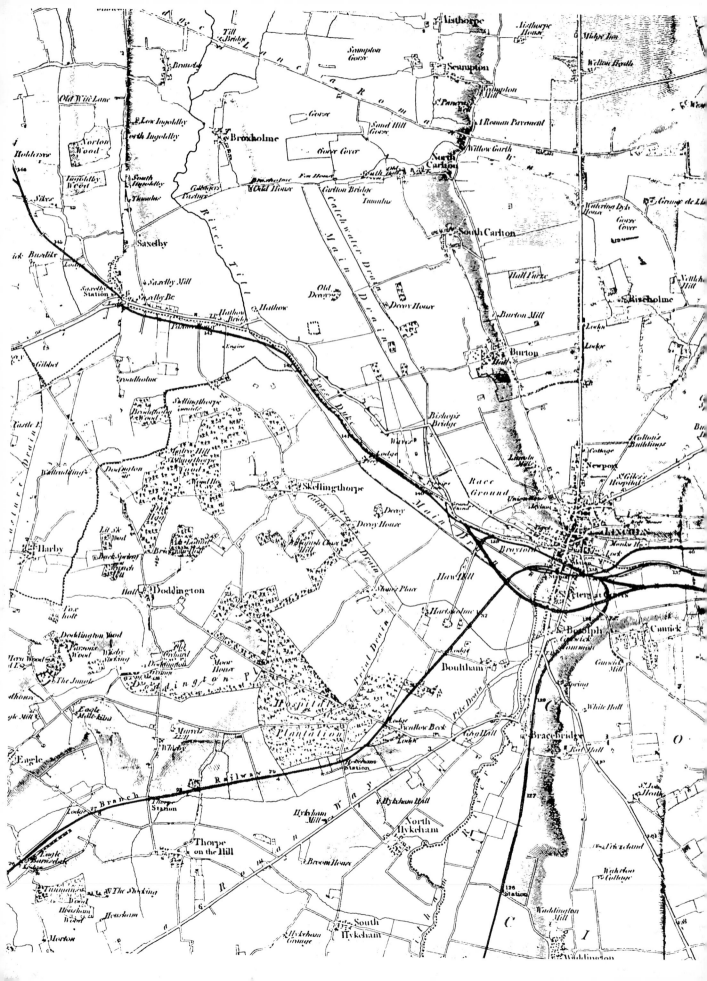